M000216306

Elena's
FAMOUS MEXICAN
and
SPANISH RECIPES

By ELENA ZELAYETA

Edited by

A GROUP OF SAN FRANCISCO HOME ECONOMISTS

Art Work by

PHILIP LITTLE AND NORMAN GORDON

The *Vintage Cookery Books* Series

A Short History of the Cook Book

One might be forgiven for thinking, in our age of celebrity chefs and glossy publications, that cook books are a relatively modern occurrence. However cook books have an incredibly long history, dating as far back as the first century CE.

The oldest collection of recipes that has survived in Europe is *De Re Coquinaria*, written in Latin. An early version was first compiled sometime in the first century and has often been attributed to the Roman gourmet, Marcus Gavius Apicius. An even earlier example (though less recognisable as a modern cook book), was also found in the Roman empire. This was the first known food writer – a Greek Sicilian named Archestratus, who lived in the fourth century BCE. He wrote a poem that spoke of using 'top quality and seasonal' ingredients, and insisted that flavours should not be masked by spices, herbs or other seasonings. Archestratus placed special importance on the simple preparation of fish.

Simplicity was abandoned and replaced by a culture of gastronomy as the Roman Empire developed however. By the time *De Re Coquinaria* was published, it contained 470 recipes calling for heavy use of spices and herbs. After a long interval, the first recipe books to be compiled in Europe since Late Antiquity started to appear in the thirteenth century. About a hundred are known to have survived, some fragmentary, from the age before printing. The earliest genuinely medieval recipes have been found in a Danish manuscript dating from around

1300, which in turn is a copy of older texts that date back to the early thirteenth century or perhaps earlier. Chinese cook books have also been found, dating to around this time – and one of the earliest surviving Chinese-language cookbooks; Hu Sihui's *Important Principles of Food and Drink* is believed to have been written in 1330.

German manuscripts are among the most numerous examples of cook books, among them being *The Book of Good Food* written in 1350 and *Kitchen Mastery* written in 1485. Two French collections are probably the most famous: *Le Viandier* ('The Provisioner') which was compiled in the late fourteenth century by Guillaume Tirel, and *The Householder of Paris*; a household book written by an anonymous middle class Parisian in the 1390s. Recipes originating in England include the earliest recorded recipe for ravioli, and the renowned *Forme of Cury* (mid-fourteenth century), compiled by the Master Cooks of King Richard II of England.

Cookbooks that serve as basic kitchen references (sometimes known as 'kitchen bibles') began to appear in the early modern period. They provided not just recipes but overall instructions for both kitchen technique and household management. Such books were written primarily for housewives and occasionally domestic servants, as opposed to professional cooks. Containing a veritable wealth of information, books such as *The Joy of Cooking* (USA), *La Bonne Cuisine de Madame E. Saint-Ange* (France), *The Art of Cookery* (UK), *Il Cucchiaio D'Argento* (Italy), and *A Gift to Young Housewives* (Russia) have served as records for entire national cuisines. With the advent of the printing press in the sixteenth and seventeenth centuries, numerous books were written on how to manage households and prepare food. In Holland and England especially, competition grew between the noble families as to who could prepare the most lavish banquet.

By the 1660s, cookery had progressed to an art form and good cooks were in demand. Many of these professional chefs took full advantage of the new trend, and published their own books detailing their recipes in competition with their rivals. By the nineteenth century, the Victorian preoccupation for domestic respectability brought about the emergence of cookery writing in its modern form. Although eclipsed in fame and regard by Isabella Beeton, the first modern cookery writer and compiler of recipes for the home was Eliza Acton. Her pioneering cookbook, *Modern Cookery for Private Families* (published in 1845), was aimed at the domestic reader rather than the professional cook or chef. This was an immensely influential book, and it established the format for modern writing about cookery.

The publication of *Modern Cookery* introduced the now-universal practice of listing the ingredients and suggested cooking times with each recipe. It also included the first recipe for Brussels sprouts. The book long survived its author, remaining in print until 1914 – functioning as an important influence on Isabella Beeton. Beeton went on to write and publish *Mrs Beeton's Book of Household Management* in twenty-four monthly parts between 1857 and 1861. Of the 1,112 pages detailing domestic issues, over 900 contained recipes, such that another popular name for the volume is *Mrs Beeton's Cookbook*. Most of the recipes were illustrated with coloured engravings, and it was the first book to show recipes in a format that is still used today. In 1896, the American cook Fannie Farmer published her illustrious work, *The Boston Cooking School Cookbook*, which contained some 1,849 recipes.

A good store of vintage cook books should be a kitchen staple for any creative cook. And as such, this series provides a collection of works, designed to instruct, inform and entertain the modern-day reader on times, peoples and foods of the past.

Today, the simple pleasures of practical household skills (so wonderfully demonstrated in these books) have been all but forgotten. Now, it's time to get back to basics. This series will take the reader back to the golden age of practical skills; an age where making and mending, cooking and preserving, brewing and bottling, were all done within the home.

The *Vintage Cookery Books* series hopes to bring old wisdom and classic techniques back to life, as we have so much to learn from 'the old ways' of cooking. Not only can these books provide a fascinating window into past societies, cultures and every-day life, but they also let us actively delve into our own history – with a taste of what, how and when, people ate, drank, and socialised. Enjoy.

INTRODUCING ELENA

I wish I had the power to let you know my friend Elena as I know her. First, let me tell you Elena is blind. Not the blindness that evokes pity, for Elena is a bouncing ball of pep, gaiety, kindliness and heart—a heart so big it encompasses all she meets.

Elena, born in Mexico City, spent her childhood in the little mining town *El Mineral del Oro* (The Gold Mine) where her parents were the village innkeepers. It was in this setting Elena learned the magic of foods.

Ten years ago, after she had come with her parents to the United States, had married, borne two sons, and owned her own restaurant, she lost her sight.

Those were tragic days for Elena, days of bitterness, financial worry, groping in the darkness. Then she began to think. She made up her mind she would not penalize her loved ones for her misfortune. To this tremendous problem she applied the same determination that she had used in overcoming other obstacles—the depression, for example, when her magic cooking fingers had helped them through.

To know real happiness you should know Elena. She is truly one of those "keepers of dreams" of whom and to whom Don Blanding speaks in his poignant poem, "To The Blind":

What is the secret of your quiet smiles?
Do you with shuttered eyes see true reality
While we see only tinted surfaces?
Do you see Spring herself
While we see only her bright garments?
Do you see hearts
While we see only faces that are masks?
Do you, in the calm silences of twilight, see God
While we but sense His presence?

You are the Keepers of Dreams.
Guard them well.
We need them,
And we need you!

This book of her own much-used recipes is just one expression of Elena's love of people, her knowledge of how to make them happy. Each recipe is a shining star of courage, faith and hope, plus a full measure of gastronomic enjoyment for you who use them.—KATHERINE KERRY.

Don Blanding's poem printed by permission of Dodd, Mead and Company

TABLE OF CONTENTS

The recipes in this book represent my conception of Mexican food as we like it best here in the United States, as observed during my years of experience in the restaurant business. In other words, along with giving recipes for traditional Mexican dishes, I have included many American adaptations — easy to prepare, easy to serve. All recipes have been thoroughly tested, all carry my wishes for *Buena suerte!*—ELENA.

Chapter One
SOPAS - Soups

CAMARON QUE SE DUERME SE LO LLEVA LA CORRIENTE
(Don't go to sleep or the parade will pass you by.)

SOPAS—Soups

TWO TYPES of soups are served in Mexico. One is the liquid soup which is served at the beginning of the meal; the other is the dry soup which comes on right after the liquid one. These dry soups are usually made of rice or vermicelli, cooked in soup stock, the stock being entirely absorbed in cooking. For the ordinary meal only one soup is served, but for a party dinner there must be both kinds. Do I hear some of you say, "But some of those soup recipes would take half a day to prepare!" Yes, it is true, many Mexican soups do require time and work to get ready. But try them, anyway. They're really delicious!

SOPA JULIANA CON ALBONDIGAS
Vegetable Soup with Meatballs

4 tablespoons oil
1 onion, minced
¼ cup tomato sauce
3 quarts chicken stock
2 large carrots
1 pound fresh peas
½ pound string beans

3 tablespoons raw rice
½ pound ground pork
½ pound ground beef
6 mint leaves
¼ cup parsley
1 egg, slightly beaten
1 teaspoon salt
Pepper

Fry onion in oil about 5 minutes, then add tomato sauce and stock. When mixture is boiling add cubed vegetables. Prepare meat as follows: Mix rice into meat, adding chopped parsley and mint leaves and salt and pepper. Add egg and mix well. Roll mixture into small balls the size of a pecan, and drop into boiling stock. Cover tightly and let simmer half an hour. Serves 6 to 8.

9

SOPA DE ALBONDIGAS
Meatball Soup

Broth
1 onion, minced
1 clove garlic, minced
¼ cup oil
½ can tomato sauce
3 quarts beef stock
Sprig of mint leaves

Albondigas
¾ pound ground beef
¾ pound ground pork
⅓ cup raw rice
1½ teaspoons salt
¼ teaspoon pepper
1 egg, slightly beaten

Fry minced onion and garlic in oil; add tomato sauce and beef stock. Heat to boiling point. Mix meat with rice, egg, and salt and pepper, and shape into little balls. Drop into boiling broth. Cover tightly, and cook 30 minutes. Add sprig of mint about 10 minutes before soup is done. Serves 6 to 8.

SOPA DE ESPUMA
Foam Soup

½ cube butter (¼ cup)
¾ cup flour
½ teaspoon baking powder
2 eggs

2 tablespoons grated cheese
5 quarts well-seasoned
  chicken broth
½ can tomato sauce

Melt butter over warm water. Add flour and baking powder sifted together. Add one egg at a time and mix well, then add the cheese. Drop this mixture by teaspoonfuls into the boiling broth which has been combined with the tomato sauce, and cook 10 minutes without uncovering. Serves 6 to 8. This is called "foam soup" because the tiny dumplings are light as foam.

SOPA DE BOLITAS DE LECHE
Soup with Custard Balls

Custard Balls
3 cups milk
3 egg yolks
¾ cup flour
Salt and pepper

Broth
½ an onion, minced
3 tablespoons butter
¼ cup tomato puree
1 cup fresh peas
1 large potato, diced
3 quarts chicken or beef stock

Custard Balls: Heat 2 cups milk in double boiler. Beat egg yolks, and stir in flour and cold milk, making a smooth paste. Add to hot milk and cook, stirring, until smoothly thickened. Season to taste with salt and pepper. Let cool, then flour hands and shape the cold custard into balls the size of a large cherry. Dip into flour and let stand a couple of hours, then fry quickly in deep hot fat; place as many balls as wished in each soup plate, and pour boiling hot broth over them.

Broth: Fry minced onion in butter for a few minutes. Add tomato, peas and potato; then add chicken broth. Cook until vegetables are tender. Serves 6 to 8.

To make tomato puree (which is called for in many of these recipes) force solid pack canned tomatoes through a sieve. When a recipe calls for tomato sauce, it means the canned variety.

SOPA DE PAPA
Potato Soup

3 large potatoes
¼ cup oil
½ cup chopped celery
½ medium onion, minced
¼ cup tomato puree
2 quarts chicken or beef stock
Salt and pepper

Peel and slice potatoes into rings. Fry in oil with celery and onion about 5 minutes. Add tomato puree and broth. Cook until potatoes are tender. Season to taste and serve with grated cheese. Serves 6 to 8.

SOPA DE BOLITAS DE PAPA
Potato Ball Soup

½ an onion, minced
¼ cup puree tomatoes
4 tablespoons oil
3 quarts beef or chicken stock
3 large potatoes
2 tablespoons butter
3 to 4 tablespoons grated cheese
Salt and pepper

Fry onion and tomato in oil. Add broth and season well. Cook potatoes and mash, adding butter, seasoning, and grated cheese. Make into small balls, placing as many as desired in each soup plate. Then pour on hot broth. Serves 6.

SOPA DE AJO
Garlic Soup

2 cloves garlic
⅓ cup oil, preferably olive oil
3 slices French bread (cubed)
½ teaspoon paprika
1 quart broth
Salt and pepper
4 to 6 eggs (1 per person)

Mince garlic and brown in oil. Add bread cubes and toss them in the oil, then add paprika and broth. Season to taste. Cook 15 minutes; when almost ready to serve, break into the broth as many eggs as desired, and poach. Serve soup with an egg in each plate. Serves 4 to 6.

SOPA DE LENTEJAS
Lentil Soup

1 pound lentils
3 quarts water
1 onion, minced
2 cloves of garlic, minced

½ cup tomato sauce
¼ cup oil
Salt and pepper
3 slices bacon, minced

Wash lentils and put into a kettle that can be tightly covered. Add other ingredients, heat to boiling, then lower temperature and let simmer 2 hours. Serves 6 to 8.

SOPA DE FRIJOL
Bean Soup

1 pound Mexican pink
beans
2 quarts lukewarm water
1 onion, minced
1 clove garlic, minced

1 teaspoon oregano
Salt and pepper
½ cup tomato sauce
3 tablespoons oil

Cook all ingredients, with the exception of the tomato sauce and oil, slowly until beans are very tender, approximately 2 hours. When beans are cold, mash pulp through strainer, add the liquid and set aside. Fry tomato sauce in oil, add bean mixture and cook 15 minutes longer. Serve with croutons and grated cheese. Serves 6.

SOPA DE GARBANZO
Chick Pea Soup

1 pound garbanzos
½ pound salt pork
1 onion, minced
2 cloves garlic, minced

½ cup oil
2 quarts lukewarm water
Salt and pepper to taste

Cover garbanzos with lukewarm water, add 1 teaspoon salt and soak overnight. Drain and combine with all the other ingredients. Cover and cook approximately 2 hours, or until garbanzos are well done. The garbanzos may be served in this manner, or they may be pureed as the bean soup and served with croutons. Makes 6 servings.

SOPA DE CEBOLLA ESTILO ALDEANO
Onion Soup, Peasant Style

4 large onions
¼ cup butter
4 tablespoons flour

1 quart strong broth
3 cups milk
1 cup cream

Chop onions and simmer in the butter 30 minutes in a covered kettle. Stir often and do not let onions brown. Stir in flour. Mix well and add strong broth (mixture of chicken and beef is best). Allow to simmer for 20 minutes, add milk and cream. Heat to boiling point, season and serve. To serve, spread 6 slices of toasted French bread with ½ cup grated Parmesan cheese, blended with 2 well-beaten egg yolks. Place in soup tureen and pour over them the boiling broth. Cover tureen at once with lid and let stand 3 or 4 minutes before serving. Serves 6.

SOPA DE GLOBITOS
Mock Garbanzo Soup

4 eggs	½ a minced onion
2 cups flour, or more if	¼ cup tomato puree
needed	3 quarts chicken or beef
½ cup butter	broth
1 cup milk	Salt and pepper

Mix eggs, flour, melted butter and milk to make a soft dough. Knead and make into tiny balls, size of garbanzos. Fry lightly in a little oil, and set aside while you make the broth: Fry onion and tomato in oil. Add well-seasoned broth. Drop in balls and cook for 15 to 20 minutes, or until done. Serves 6.

SOPA RANCHERA
Ranch-Style Soup

1 medium-sized onion,	3 quarts chicken broth
finely minced	½ cup uncooked rice
4 tablespoons oil	1 pound fresh peas
½ cup tomato puree	Salt and pepper

Brown onion in oil. Add tomato puree and cook for a few minutes, then add chicken broth. When stock is boiling, add rice and peas, cover tightly and cook slowly 30 minutes. When ready to serve, pieces of chicken may be added if desired. Serves 6.

SOPA DE ELOTE CON ESPARRAGOS
Corn Soup with Asparagus

2 tablespoons minced onion	1 No. 2 can cream-style
½ cup butter (1 cube)	corn
1 quart milk	1 pound green asparagus
	Salt and pepper

Fry onion in butter until soft, add milk, corn, and asparagus which has been cleaned and cut into inch pieces. Add salt and pepper to taste and cook, covered, until asparagus is tender. This may be varied by using diced potato instead of asparagus. Serves 4 to 6.

MENUDO
Tripe Soup

2 calves feet
6 quarts water
5 pounds tripe
3 cups hominy
3 onions, minced

4 cloves garlic, minced
1 tablespoon oregano
2 teaspoons cilantro
Salt and pepper

Wash calves feet, add water and cook 1 hour. Wash tripe, cut in pieces about 1 by 2 inches and add to calves feet. Add hominy, onion and garlic. Add spices which have been tied loosely in a cheesecloth bag, and let simmer 6 to 7 hours. The proper way to serve this dish is with minced green onions and minced mint leaves. Splendid for large parties. (Serves 12.) Good served with red chili sauce from Mexican store.

SOPA DE SESOS
Calf Brain Soup

½ an onion, minced
¼ cup butter
2 large potatoes
3 large leeks

2 quarts beef stock
2 pairs calves brains
Grated cheese

Fry onion in butter; add cubed potatoes and leeks and cook for approximately 5 minutes. Add broth and simmer approximately 30 minutes. Cook brains in gently boiling salted water for 15 minutes. Plunge into ice water to cool, then remove membranes, trim and slice. Place slices on top of soup, heat, and sprinkle with grated cheese. Serves 6.

SOPA DE BUNUELOS
Vegetable Soup with Wafers

1 cup flour
2 tablespoons butter or
   other shortening
½ teaspoon salt

3 egg yolks
⅓ cup water
Chicken broth

First make wafers: sift flour, add salt, work in butter as for pie crust, then stir in egg yolks beaten with water, and mix to make a soft dough. Roll out thin on floured board and cut into small fancy shapes as desired. Fry in hot oil until gold colored. Place layer of wafers in tureen. Sprinkle with grated cheese, followed by rings of cooked Italian squash, rings of cooked carrots and cooked peas (all thoroughly heated). Continue to alternate layers of wafers and vegetables until all are used. Pour over them well seasoned chicken broth, and serve very hot.

SOPA DE ALBONDIGAS DE PESCADO
Fishball Soup

1 large halibut head and trimmings	8 whole black peppers (peppercorns)
3 quarts water	1 bay leaf
1 large onion	Salt and pepper
2 cloves garlic	1/4 cup tomato puree
1 tablespoon oregano	2 large potatoes, cubed

Simmer the first 8 ingredients together about 30 minutes, until a rich broth has been made. Strain. Cook the tomato puree and potatoes in oil for 5 minutes and add the strained broth. Let simmer while you make the fish balls as follows:

1 1/2 pounds halibut	1 teaspoon oregano
2 eggs, beaten	Salt and pepper

Remove bones and grind raw halibut; add remaining ingredients and mix well. Roll into balls about the size of a walnut. Drop into boiling broth and cook, tightly covered, 30 minutes. Serves 6 to 8.

SOPA DE PESCADO A LA ESPANOLA
Fish Soup, Spanish Style

1 1/2 pounds sliced halibut	2 tablespoons minced parsley
4 tablespoons oil (preferably olive oil)	5 cups water
	1 slice bread
1 onion, minced	1/3 cup blanched almonds
1 clove garlic, minced	1/4 cup filberts
	Salt and pepper

Salt fish, roll in flour and brown in oil; remove from pan. In the remaining oil, fry onion and garlic about 5 minutes; add parsley, water, and pieces of fish from which bones have been removed. In another saucepan fry bread, almonds, and filberts in a little oil, remove, grind to a fine paste and add to broth. Season with salt and pepper. Serves 4.

SOPA DE ALMEJAS A LA ESPANOLA
Clam Soup, Spanish Style

2 1/2 dozen clams	2 cloves garlic, minced
1 large onion, minced	1/4 cup minced parsley
4 tablespoons olive oil	1/2 cup tomato puree

Wash clams thoroughly, cover with boiling salted water and cook until shells open; remove from shells. (If large, chop coarsely.) Strain juice through cheesecloth to remove sand. Fry onion and garlic in oil, then add parsley and tomato puree. Now add clams and broth, season with salt and pepper to taste, and heat thoroughly. Serves 4.

SOPA DE TORTILLA
Tortilla Soup

4 tortillas
¼ cup oil
1 onion, chopped
½ cup tomato puree
3 quarts broth, chicken
or beef

1 teaspoon cilantro
(coriander)
Sprig mint leaves
Grated cheese

Cut tortillas into strips about the size of macaroni. Fry tortillas in oil until crisp, then remove from pan and drain on absorbent paper. Place in pot and add boiling broth which has been prepared in the following manner: Fry onion and tomato puree in the oil which was used in frying the tortillas. Add stock. Mash the cilantro, add a little broth, and strain into the stock. Cook half an hour, adding the mint leaves during the last 10 minutes. Serve with grated cheese. Serves 6.

SOPA SECA DE ARROZ CON JAMON
Dry Rice Soup with Ham

1 cup uncooked rice
1 clove garlic
½ cup oil
2 tablespoons minced onion

3 tablespoons tomato sauce
1 pound smoked ham
2¼ cups boiling water
Salt and pepper to taste

Brown clove garlic in oil; remove from pan and throw away. Fry rice until golden brown. Add minced onion, tomato, and ham which has been cut into cubes and fried separately. Add boiling water, season, and cover tightly. Cook slowly for 30 minutes. Do not peek before the time is up. Serves 6. This dish may be varied by using, instead of the ham, pork sausages cut into pieces, or peas, or wet pack shrimps, saving the water of the shrimps and using as part of the 2¼ cups of water called for.

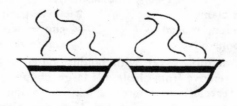

SOPA DE TAQUITOS
Pancake Soup

½ can tomato sauce
3 tablespoons oil
2 quarts meat stock

12 small thin pancakes
2 hard-cooked eggs, chopped

Add tomato sauce to oil and cook a few minutes, add stock and let simmer. When almost ready to serve, make pancakes, following your favorite pancake recipe. Spread hot pancakes with one of these fillings: (1) butter and grated cheese; (2) well-seasoned cooked vegetables; (3) well-seasoned chopped cooked chicken. Roll up and place 3 filled pancakes in each soup plate, add broth and sprinkle chopped hard-cooked eggs over all. Serves 4.

SOPA DE FIDEO
Dry Vermicelli Soup

½ pound vermicelli
   (3 strands)
½ cup oil
½ an onion, minced

2 fresh tomatoes, peeled
2 cups chicken broth
Salt and pepper

Fry vermicelli in hot oil until golden brown in color; remove from pan. In same oil fry minced onion, add chopped tomato. Add chicken broth, season, and when broth is boiling add vermicelli. Cook, covered, until dry—approximately 30 minutes. Serve sprinkled with grated cheese. Serves 4.

SOPA SECA DE TORTILLA
Dry Tortilla Soup

6 tortillas
½ cup oil
1 onion, minced
2 cups tomato puree
6 hard-cooked eggs

1 bay leaf
1 teaspoon oregano
Salt and pepper to taste
Grated cheese

Cut tortillas into strips like macaroni. Fry in oil until crisp. Set aside to drain on brown paper. Fry minced onion in oil in which tortillas were fried. Add tomato puree. Season and cook, covered, 30 minutes. Butter a casserole. Place in layers, tortilla strips, sauce, grated cheese, and round slices of hard-cooked eggs. Follow same procedure until all ingredients are used, having rounds of eggs for last layer. Cover with remaining sauce. Bake in moderate oven (350°) 30 minutes. Serves 6.

These dry soups also make good entrees.

17

TWO
COMPANY DINNERS
AND HOW
TO MANAGE THEM

●

SOPA DE ESPUMA (Foam Soup)
CHILES RELLENOS (Cheese Stuffed Peppers)
TOSTADAS
(Crisp Fried Tortillas with Vegetables and Chorizo)
FRIJOLES REFRITOS (Refried Beans)
FLAN (Caramel Custard)   Coffee

This is an easy dinner to prepare and serve for you can have
everything done in advance, needing only a few finishing touches.
The soup with dumplings can be all ready simply to reheat and
serve; the *Chiles Rellenos* stuffed and fried the day before, to be
reheated for a few minutes in the sauce; the beans cooked and fried,
ready to refry; the Flan made and cooled (not in the refrigerator).
No salad is needed because lettuce and vegetables are used in the
Tostadas. And here's a secret — this is really a very inexpensive
company dinner.

SOPA DE ALBONDIGAS (Mexican Meat Ball Soup)
TACOS DE JOCOQUI (Rolled Tortillas with Sour Cream)
FRIJOLES REFRITOS (Refried Beans)
ENSALADA JARDINERA (Garden Salad)
BUDIN DE PLATANO A LA MEXICANA (Mexican
Banana Pudding)
Coffee

Here again the preparations can be done well in advance, so that
you can be free to be a hostess rather than a flurried cook. The
soup with its meat balls can be cooked the day before, needing
only to be reheated at the proper time; the tortillas filled and
rolled, ready to have the sour cream poured over them before
baking; the salad things prepared for last minute mixing; and the
pudding baked and chilled. A menu of this type is an excellent one
for serving to large groups.

Recipes for all dishes called for are given in this book.

18

Chapter Two

HUEVOS - Eggs

MAS VALE LLEGAR A TIEMPO QUE SER INVITADO. (It is better to drop in at the right time than to be invited.)

HUEVOS—Eggs

*I*N MEXICO *the egg is really a good egg for it is glorified and made into all sorts of wonderful dishes with good-tasting sauces. I think we might well do the same for eggs here in the United States. If the combinations given in this chapter seem too hot or too complicated for breakfast eating, try them for lunch or supper. I'm sure you'll like them.*

TORTILLA DE HUEVO A LA ESPANOLA
Spanish Omelet

Sauce	Omelets
1 small onion, minced	8 eggs (2 for each omelet)
3 tablespoons oil	8 tablespoons milk (2 for
1 bell pepper, chopped fine	each omelet)
2 cups tomato puree	Salt and pepper

Make the sauce first: Fry the onion in hot oil, then add pepper and tomato puree. Cook for 20 minutes. Add salt and pepper to taste. Makes sauce enough for 4 omelets. If desired a little chili powder may be added. Make omelet in the usual way, adding the milk when beating the eggs, and seasoning to taste with salt and pepper. Serve on a hot plate dressed with the sauce.

TORTILLA CON HUEVO
Tortilla with Egg

1 tortilla (bought in Mexican store)	2 eggs
3 tablespoons oil	Salt to taste

Cut tortilla into eighths and fry in oil, not too crisp. Beat eggs, adding salt, and pour over fried tortilla, turning as you would an omelet. This makes a delightful dish. Serves 1 or 2.

HUEVOS REVUELTOS A LA MEXICANA
Mexican Scrambled Eggs

3 tablespoons minced onion	½ cup tomato puree
1 clove garlic, minced	¼ cup water
2 green peppers, finely chopped	Salt and pepper to taste
3 tablespoons butter	6 eggs, slightly beaten

Fry onion, garlic and green pepper in butter. Then add tomato puree, water, and salt and pepper to taste. Cook for 3 minutes; then add lightly beaten eggs, and scramble. Serves 3 or 4.

NIDOS DE ARROZ CON HUEVO
Rice Nests with Egg

¼ cup butter	6 slices bacon
1½ cups cooked white rice	6 eggs
¼ cup milk	Salt and pepper

Butter baking pan and make 6 nests of cooked rice. Fry bacon, but not crisp, and place around rice nests, holding in place with toothpick. Break an egg into each nest, sprinkle with salt and pepper, and dot with butter. Bake at 375° until white of egg is cooked, but yolk is still tender. Takes 5 to 7 minutes. Serves 6.

HUEVOS RANCHEROS
Eggs Ranch Style

1 clove garlic	3 tablespoons oil
1 teaspoon oregano	1 cup tomato sauce
Chile tepines to taste (I use 2)	Salt and pepper
1 cup tomato puree (strained)	2 eggs per person

Mash very well garlic, oregano and chile tepines. Mix with tomato puree and strain. Fry in oil, adding tomato sauce and seasoning. The eggs may be fried separately, and the sauce poured over them, or they may be poached right in the sauce.

HUEVOS VERDES, BLANCOS Y COLORADOS
Eggs, Green, White and Red

¼ cup butter	Salt and pepper
3 tablespoons minced parsley	6 slices fresh tomatoes
6 eggs	

Butter custard cups well; sprinkle parsley in bottom of each cup; break one egg into each, being careful not to break yolk. Season with salt and pepper, and dot with butter. Bake in a moderately hot oven (375°) 12 to 15 minutes. If eggs are to be served cold, season slices of tomato with oil and vinegar and scoop an egg out onto each slice. If preferred, the eggs may be served hot on square slices of bread fried in butter. Tomato sauce may be poured over the eggs if desired. Serves 6.

HUEVOS AL HORNO A LA MEXICANA
Shirred Eggs Mexican Style

½ an onion, minced

2 tablespoons butter

1 can tomato sauce

3 or more chile tepines, as desired

Salt and pepper

6 eggs

Fry onion in butter until tender, but do not brown. Add tomato sauce, mashed chiles, and a small amount of water if sauce is very thick. Add salt and pepper to taste. Divide sauce into 6 greased custard cups, and break one egg into each cup. Place cups in a pan of hot water and bake from 12 to 15 minutes in a 375° oven. These may be scooped out of the cups and served over white rice or toast. Makes 6 servings.

JINETE A CABALLO CON CHAPARRERAS
Tostadas with Fried Eggs

6 raspadas (unfried tostadas from Mexican store)

2 tablespoons oil

12 eggs, fried

½ teaspoon oregano

1 clove garlic

3 or more chile tepines, if desired—they're hot!

2 cups tomato puree

Salt and pepper

Fry raspadas in oil until golden and very crisp. Set aside to drain on absorbent paper. Place 2 fried eggs on each tostada (the raspadas are tostadas now that they have been fried!) and bathe with the following sauce: Mash very well the oregano, garlic and chile tepines; add a little water and strain. Add to tomato puree. Heat oil and add sauce to it. Add salt and pepper to taste. Cook for 15 minutes and pour over eggs on tostadas. Makes 6 servings.

A TYPICAL MEXICAN DINNER
SOPA SECA DE ARROZ CON JAMON
(Dry Rice Soup with Ham)
POLLO A LA PLAZA (Mexican Country Style Chicken)
FRIJOLES REFRITOS (Refried Beans) RASPADAS
BUDIN DE PAN Y NARANJA (Orange Bread Pudding)
Coffee

A dry soup such as the one called for in this menu may be served in soup plates or cereal dishes, and eaten with either a spoon or a fork. The chicken is best served on individual dinner plates; the refried beans on a platter, to be passed at table. The raspadas are cut in quarters, fried crisp, and served hot, to take the place of bread.

FIESTA MENUS

•

FESTIVE MEXICAN DINNER

GUACAMOLE with Sliced Tomatoes (may be served with
main course)

SOPA DE CEBOLLA ESTILO ALDEANA
(Onion Soup, Peasant Style)

POLLO EN MOLE VERDE (Chicken in Green Mole Sauce)

FRIJOLES REFRITOS (Refried Beans)

RASPADAS (cut in quarters and fried crisp)

COCADA (Coconut Pudding)   Coffee

Spread the table with a red and white checked tablecloth with
matching napkins. For a centerpiece use a wooden bowl filled with
colorful vegetables and tropical fruits (such as pineapple, bananas,
etc.) letting them overflow onto the table. For most effective place
cards sew or paste a miniature tamale to a corner of each card.
Make the tamales by cutting two-inch squares of corn husk or
crepe paper, fill with cotton, and tie at both ends with three strands
of narrow ribbon in the Mexican national colors, green, white, red.

•

MEXICAN LUNCHEON

Salad of Avocado Stuffed with Fruit

CHILE CON QUESO (Green Chile with Cheese)

FRIJOLES REFRITOS (Refried Beans)   Hot Tortillas

BUDIN DE PAN CON SALSA DE CARAMELO
(Bread Pudding with Caramel Sauce)

Coffee

Use a Mexican tablecloth. In the center arrange green, white and
red carnations in a white bowl (dip white carnations in green dye
to make them green). Place cards may be purchased in a Mexican
curio shop; or little figures such as the sombrero, cactus and the
like used in this book, may be drawn on cards, or cut out of folded
paper and stood at each place.

Chapter Three

PESCADOS - Fish

CUANDO DOS SE QUIEREN BIEN, CON UNO QUE COMA BASTA.
(When a couple are in love, if only one eats, it should be sufficient.)

25

PESCADOS—Fish

I HAVE BEEN *asked a good many times if fish is eaten freely in Mexico. The answer is "yes," and each locality has its own special favorites. In Baja California, you get abalone, sardines, mackerel, and tuna. In Sonora, deep water fish such as sail fish, sword fish, totoaba and cabrilla. When you go to Guaymas you'll be served oysters; in Sinaloa, shrimps and prawns; at Mazatlan, large fish such as mero and pargo, and, of course, the popular "lisa" which is barbecued and sold whole in the market places. In Mexico City (where I was born) much fish and sea food is shipped in from various sections of the country, with the result that one can get almost any kind of fish at any time of the year — including the baby octopus, which is really wonderful when made into soup.*

CACEROLA DE BACALAO A LA ESPANOLA
Codfish Casserole, Spanish

1 pound codfish	1 pound fresh tomatoes, peeled
½ cup oil, preferably olive oil	4 bell peppers
1 large onion, cut in rings	Salt and pepper to taste

Soak codfish overnight; cut into cubes and cook until tender. In the oil, saute onion rings, then add tomatoes which have been chopped. Season with salt and pepper. Butter casserole well, place layer of codfish, then a layer of bell peppers which have been skinned by placing under the broiler, turning on all sides until skin blisters, then placed in paper bag to steam. (Remove seeds of peppers and cut peppers in strips). Over the codfish and peppers pour some of the tomato mixture; repeat this procedure until all ingredients have been used. Bake in a moderate oven (350°) for 45 minutes. Serves 4 to 6.

BACALAO A LA VIZCAINA
Codfish, Spanish Style

1 pound salt codfish
1 large onion, minced
2 cloves garlic, minced
½ cup olive oil

2 cups tomato puree
1 can pimientos
Salt and pepper

Soak codfish overnight in cold water to cover. Drain and shred. Fry onion, garlic and codfish in the oil about 5 minutes. Add tomato puree and ½ cup of the water in which the codfish was soaked. Cook slowly, well covered, until codfish is tender, adding the cut pimientos about 10 minutes before codfish is done. If desired, green olives may also be used. Be careful not to add too much salt, as codfish is salty in itself. Serves 4 to 6.

BACALAO ARRIERO A LA ESPANOLA
Spanish Codfish, Country Style

1 pound salt codfish
6 cloves garlic
⅓ cup oil
1 pound tomatoes, peeled

1 can pimientos, cut in strips
1 egg, beaten
Salt and pepper

Soak codfish overnight in cold water to cover. Brown garlic in very hot oil and remove. To the oil add chopped tomatoes, pimientos and codfish. Cook about 20 minutes, covered. When ready to serve, stir in well-beaten egg, season, and serve at once. Serves 6.

ATUN EN ESCABECHE
Pickled Tuna Fish

5 pounds tuna fish, sliced
2 cups oil
3 large onions, cut in rings
5 cloves garlic

1 pint vinegar
4 bay leaves
1 tablespoon whole black
    pepper
Salt to taste

Salt slices of fish and fry until brown in the oil. Place in a crockery jar or earthenware casserole in layers. When all the fish has been fried, fry onion and garlic in same oil about 5 minutes. Add vinegar, bay leaves and whole pepper, heat to boiling and pour at once over fish. If fish is not well covered add more vinegar. This fish should not be eaten until at least 24 hours after it is made, for the flavor improves as time goes on. It will keep indefinitely and is grand for the winter shelf. When tuna fish is raw, it is rather mushy, but this does not indicate that the fish is spoiled. You will find that it becomes firm as you fry it.

PESCADO EN SALSA VERDE
Fish in Green Sauce

1 pound fresh long green chiles	½ cup oil
2 pounds bell peppers	2 cloves garlic, peeled
1 large onion	2 tablespoons flour
1 cup parsley	1 sea bass or striped bass
	Salt and pepper to taste

Place chiles and peppers under broiler, turning on all sides until skin blisters. Place in a paper bag, close and let steam for 15 minutes, then peel. Remove seeds, grind peppers, chiles, onions and parsley in food grinder. Heat oil, in it brown whole cloves of garlic and remove from pan. To the hot oil add flour and brown, then add the chile mixture. Season with salt and pepper and let sauce cook until oil comes to the top. In an oiled baking pan put the cleaned fish and sprinkle with salt and pepper and a little oil. Bake uncovered until tender, about 45 minutes to an hour. Remove fish to hot platter, including the hot liquid that has formed in the pan. Remove bones (if desired), then pour the hot sauce over the fish. Serves 6.

TORTAS DE CAMARON
Shrimp Fritters, Mexican Style

1 can wet pack shrimps (save liquid)	4 eggs, separated
¾ cup dried shrimps (buy at Mexican store)	2 tablespoons flour

Chop canned shrimps, add dried shrimps, and mix well. Beat whites of eggs stiff but not dry; beat egg yolks lightly and fold into whites, then fold in the flour. Add chopped shrimps to this batter. Drop by spoonfuls into moderately hot oil or shortening about 1½ inches deep, and fry brown on both sides; remove to absorbent paper to drain. Now make sauce as follows:

2 tablespoons oil	Liquid from canned shrimps
2 tablespoons minced onion	8-oz. bottle of red chile sauce
1 clove garlic	(from Mexican store)

Fry the onion and garlic in the oil. Add shrimp liquid and the red chile sauce. Season, being careful not to add too much salt for shrimps are salty in themselves. About 5 minutes before serving, drop fritters into this sauce and heat through for a few minutes. If desired, cactus plant (nopales) may be used with these fritters. It can be bought canned and can be heated in the same sauce as the patties. If sauce is too hot with chile, it may be diluted with water to suit the taste. Serves 6.

PESCADO RELLENO
Stuffed Fish Salad

4 thick slices halibut	¼ teaspoon pepper
Boiling water to cover	1 bay leaf
1 onion	1 teaspoon oregano
1 clove garlic	Mayonnaise
1 teaspoon salt	Pimiento
	Boiled ham

Simmer halibut in water with onion, garlic, salt, pepper, bay leaf and oregano, until fish separates easily into flakes when tested with a fork. Drain and allow to cool. Carefully remove bones without breaking the fish. Place 2 slices on a platter. Pour on the stuffing (see below) then cover with other slices and place in refrigerator for about 2 hours. Cover the top with mayonnaise and decorate with pimiento, pieces of boiled ham in the shape of scales, and lettuce or parsley. When you wish to use a whole fish, striped bass is very good. Leave the head and tail on and decorate the platter so that it looks like a live fish. Serves 4 to 6.

The Stuffing

½ cup butter (1 cube)	1 pint milk
1 onion, minced	Salt and pepper
6 tablespoons flour	4 slices boiled ham, minced

Melt butter with onion, blend in flour; add milk, and cook, stirring, until smoothly thickened. Add minced ham. Season to taste with salt and pepper.

PESCADO EN MANTEQUILLA
Fish in Butter

4 medium thick slices halibut	½ cup butter
1 medium-sized onion	Juice of 2 or 3 lemons
1 bay leaf	Salt and pepper
2 potatoes, cooked in their jackets	Garnishes

Cook fish in salted water with onion and bay leaf. Peel potatoes, slice in rounds, and brown in a little oil or butter. When fish is done, place on hot platter and surround with the browned potato slices. Pour the melted butter mixed with lemon juice over all, and decorate plate with shredded lettuce, rings of lemon and slices of tomatoes. Serves 4.

Chapter Four
TORTILLAS

BIEN COCINA LA MOZA, PERO MEJOR LA BOLSA. (The maid cooks well, but the pocketbook cooks better.)

TORTILLAS

*T*HE TORTILLA *national bread of Mexico, is used as the basis of many dishes. When the Mexican housewife makes tortillas, she shapes the masa into small balls, then dampens the palms of her hands and pats each ball of meal into a very thin, flat cake the size of a salad plate. Some Mexicans use a press instead of the hands. The tortillas are then baked on an iron griddle which has been lime-treated. That is, the cold griddle is rubbed with a teaspoon of hydrated lime, then sprinkled with water and the mixture rubbed over the surface. After standing a few minutes, the griddle is shaken to remove the surplus lime, after which it is heated very hot and the tortillas cooked until done (not browned) on both sides. That's the way it's done in Old Mexico. Here in the United States—and in the larger cities of Mexico—one can go to a Mexican store and buy the tortillas ready made, ready to heat and eat. Tacos correspond to our sandwiches; they are made by rolling or folding tortillas with cheese or other filling inside. Raspadas, used for making tostadas, are thinner than tortillas.*

TACOS DE JOCOQUI
Rolled Tortillas with Sour Cream

6 tortillas	1½ cups tomato puree
½ pound Monterey cream cheese	1 pint sour cream
2 green peeled chiles, cut in strips	Salt and pepper

Fry tortillas in butter or oil. Place cubes of cheese, strips of chiles, and 2 or 3 tablespoons of tomato puree on each tortilla; sprinkle with salt and pepper. Roll and place in a shallow baking dish. Pour sour cream over all and bake, in a moderate oven (350°) for 30 minutes. Serves 6. These should be served with refried beans.

TOSTADAS
Crisp Fried Tortillas

Fry 12 raspadas in plenty of oil until gold colored and very crisp. (Raspadas are unfried tostadas—ask for them by that name in Mexican stores.) Set aside to drain on absorbent paper. Take cooked pink Mexican beans and fry in the oil, mashing as they fry. Put a layer of the mashed beans on top of each tostada, and sprinkle generously with grated cheese. Add chorizo (Mexican sausage) which has been removed from casing, crumbled, and fried; then sprinkle with shredded lettuce; serve warm with the following sauce cold or hot poured over them.

Sauce for Tostadas

1½ cups tomato puree	2 tablespoons oil
1 minced onion	1½ teaspoons salt
1 teaspoon oregano	Green peeled chiles to
1 tablespoon vinegar	taste

Combine ingredients in order given, mashing well. If desired, zucchini or string beans may be used instead of the mashed beans. Cut zucchini in rings, string beans in small pieces and cook until tender; add a tablespoon of vinegar to water in which zucchini is cooked.

TACOS DE GALLINA
Rolled Tortillas with Chicken

Cube seasoned cooked fricassee chicken and moisten with sauce as used in "Carne de Puerco con Chile Verde"—see chapter on meats. Spread this mixture on tortillas and roll, using toothpicks to keep the tortillas from opening. Fry tortillas crisp on both sides, place two on a plate, sprinkle with grated cheese and pour Tostada sauce over them (see chapter on Tortillas). Decorate with shredded lettuce and rings of avocado. Refried Mexican beans are particularly good with this dish.

When you buy tortillas, they are soft and flat. Before serving, heat them piping hot on a dry griddle. At table, tear in pieces, roll or fold, and eat with butter. If any tortillas are left over, let them cool thoroughly, then wrap in a dry cloth and store in the refrigerator; otherwise they will buckle and warp out of shape! Tortillas thus held over for a day need to be slightly dampened before reheating. To do this, dampen the hands and rub lightly over each tortilla, then heat on the griddle.

CHALUPAS
Corn Patties

1 pound masa (sold at Mexican stores)
2 tablespoons melted shortening
1 tablespoon lukewarm water
1 teaspoon salt

2 balls chorizo
Grated cheese
Shredded lettuce

Place masa in bowl; add water, melted shortening and salt. Mix well and make into balls the size of a large walnut. Pat between moistened palms of hands until they are the size of very small pancakes. Cook on both sides in an ungreased iron skillet. While still hot, pinch edges between thumb and fingers to make a border or hollow nest. Set aside. This can all be done several hours in advance of the meal. When ready to serve, dip in sauce and fry in oil; remove to platter and stuff each with some of the chorizo which has been removed from the casing and fried. Sprinkle generously with grated cheese and shredded lettuce and pour over them the same sauce called for in tostada recipe (see page 34). Makes about 10 chalupas. It's nice to garnish them with rings of radishes and to serve refried beans as a side dish.

CHILAQUILES
Tortilla Hash

6 tortillas
¼ cup oil
1 small onion, minced
1 bell pepper, chopped

2 chorizos (Mexican sausages), may be omitted
1½ cups tomato puree
Salt and pepper
½ pound Monterey cream cheese (or American cheese) cubed

Cut tortillas in eighths. Fry in oil and remove from pan. In the oil that is left, fry onions and pepper, then add tomato. Season to taste and cook, covered, 15 minutes. In a large skillet put layers of tortillas and cubed cheese until all is used; add crumbled chorizos if you are using them. Pour sauce over them and cook gently until tortillas are tender and cheese melted—about 15 minutes. Or, place in casserole and bake 20 minutes at 325°. Serves 4.

QUESADILLA
Tortilla Stuffed with Cheese

Take fresh tortillas (bought in Mexican store), place generous piece of Monterey cream cheese (or American cheese) in the center, and fold it over as you would a turnover. Pin top with toothpicks to hold. Place in hot, ungreased skillet and cook lightly, turning often until cheese is melted. Delicious with refried beans.

ENTOMATADAS
Rolled Tortillas in Tomato Sauce

2 cups tomato puree
1 medium onion, minced
½ cup oil
Salt and pepper

6 tortillas (bought in
    Mexican store)
3 chorizos (Mexican sausage)
Grated cheese

Fry onion in 2 tablespoons oil a few minutes and add tomato puree. (Remember, tomato puree is made by sieving drained, solid-pack canned tomatoes.) Season with salt and pepper. Dip tortillas in sauce, fry lightly in remaining oil, and remove to another pan. Remove jacket from chorizo, crumble meat and fry; fill tortillas with the sausage and sprinkle generously with cheese. Roll and place close together in baking pan. Pour remaining sauce over filled rolls and sprinkle with more cheese. Place in moderately hot oven (350°) about 20 minutes, until rolls and sauce are thoroughly heated. Serve with re-fried beans. Makes 6 servings.

TACOS DE CREMA
Rolled Tortillas with Tomato Cream

6 tortillas
½ pound Monterey cream
    cheese
Green peeled chiles (accord-
    ing to taste)
1 medium-sized onion,
    minced
1 clove garlic, minced

1½ cups tomato puree
1 teaspoon salt
1 teaspoon oregano
1 pint sour cream (or 1 pint
    table cream in which 2
    packages of cream cheese
    have been dissolved)

Fry tortillas lightly in oil and spread with the cheese and chiles that have been cut into strips. Roll, place in pan and over them pour the sauce: Fry onion and garlic until browned. Add tomato puree and seasonings and cook 30 minutes tightly covered. When sauce is done, add the sour cream and pour over the tortillas. Bake, covered, in moderate oven (350°) 30 minutes. Serves 6.

ENCHILADAS

8 chiles colorados (Mexican
    red chiles)
1 clove garlic
1 teaspoon oregano
1 teaspoon salt
4 tablespoons oil

Pinch of comino (cumin
    seed), if desired
6 tortillas
3 chorizos
Grated cheese
Minced onion

Remove seeds, wash and soak chiles in warm water until tender. Do not discard water. Grind chiles, garlic, oregano until consistency of paste.

Take 1½ cups of the water that the chiles were soaked in and add to paste. Add to hot oil and simmer gently about 15 minutes. Add salt and comino (use this sparingly for it's very strong!). Dip tortillas into this sauce, then fry lightly on both sides. Remove from frying pan to another pan and spread each with chorizo which has been previously skinned, crumbled and fried. Sprinkle generously with grated cheese and minced onion, then roll it up. This makes the enchilada. Pour remaining sauce over tops of enchiladas, sprinkle with remaining grated cheese; garnish with sliced hard-cooked eggs, radishes and lettuce.

Typical Mexican enchiladas are not served with a great deal of sauce; however, in my experience in cooking for American people, I have found that they like plenty of sauce and somewhat thicker than when made as above. For them I would suggest that this recipe for sauce be doubled and just before adding the paste to hot oil, brown 2 tablespoons of flour in the oil in order to thicken the sauce. Enchiladas are best enjoyed when served with beans.

PENEQUES
Corn Meal Turnovers Stuffed with Cheese
1 pound masa (fresh ground corn meal from Mexican store)
Salt and pepper to taste   ½ pound Monterey cream cheese
5 eggs, separated   2 tablespoons flour

Add salt to masa and about 1 tablespoon of water, kneading well. Divide masa into 8 balls the size of a walnut. Take each ball and pat between dampened palms of hands, making cakes the size of small pancakes, about 3 inches across. Brown on both sides in a heavy ungreased skillet on top of stove. While still hot place a piece of cheese in the center and fold over as you would a turnover, pressing the edges together with your fingers to keep the cheese from slipping out. Put aside. Beat egg whites stiff but not dry; add beaten egg yolks and fold in flour. Dip Peneques in this batter, covering well, and fry in shallow fat. Place on absorbent paper to drain. When ready to serve, heat for 10 minutes in the following sauce: Fry 2 tablespoons minced onion in 3 tablespoons oil; add 1 cup plain tomato puree and 1½ cups broth. Season with salt and pepper to taste, and add 1 teaspoon of oregano, rubbing it between the palms of your hands into the sauce. Serves 4 or 5.

TORTA AZTECA
Casserole Aztec Style

8 tortillas	Grated cheese
½ cup oil	1 pound Monterey cream
4 chorizos (Mexican	cheese
sausages)	6 hard-cooked eggs

Fry whole tortillas lightly in oil. As each is fried, set aside. Skin and crumble chorizos and fry; set aside. Cube Monterey cheese and slice hard-cooked eggs. When this is done, make sauce as follows:

1 medium-sized onion,	3 green chiles (optional)
minced	1 teaspoon oregano
¼ cup oil	1 bay leaf
3 cups tomato puree	Salt and pepper

Fry onion in oil; add tomato puree (solid-pack canned tomatoes which have been well mashed). Season with oregano, bay leaf, salt and pepper. If chiles are being used, chop and add at this time. Cook, covered, for 30 minutes. When sauce is done, place 1 tortilla in casserole and on it spread chorizo, grated cheese, Monterey cheese, 2 or 3 tablespoons of the sauce and rings of hard-cooked eggs. Repeat this procedure until all tortillas have been put into casserole; sprinkle remaining chorizos and Monterey cheese over all, and pour on remaining sauce. Bake in a moderate oven (350°) 30 to 45 minutes. To serve, cut as you would a cake. Serve with refried beans. Serves 6.

TORTILLAS DE HARINA
Flour Tortillas

4 cups flour	6 tablespoons shortening or oil
2 teaspoons salt	1 to 1¼ cups lukewarm water

Sift dry ingredients, add shortening, working it into the flour. Stir in 1 cup water and form into a ball; if necessary use more water, until bowl is clear of all dough. Knead well on floured board and make balls size of an egg. Let them stand for 15 minutes; then roll out with rolling pin until they are the size of a salad plate. Place in hot ungreased skillet or griddle on top of stove, and cook for about 2 minutes on one side, then turn to other side and cook about 1 minute longer. These are at their best when freshly made, although they may be warmed over.

38

Chapter Five

TAMALES

A LA MEJOR COCINERA SE LE VA UN TOMATE ENTERO. (The best of cooks will sooner or later pull a boner.)

TAMALES

IKE TORTILLAS, tamales are made of moist, fresh-ground Mexican cornmeal, masa. But in a tamale, the masa is spread on a corn husk, covered with a chile-seasoned filling, then rolled, tied and steamed. For those of you who live in cities and can buy the masa and husks at Mexican stores, these should be favorite recipes. For those of you who do not live near a Mexican store I give suggestions here for other ways of making tamales.

BASIC RECIPE FOR TAMALES
Basic Recipe for Masa (Corn Meal) for Tamales

5 pounds masa (fresh ground cornmeal bought in Mexican stores—do not use domestic variety)

1½ pounds shortening, preferably lard
5 teaspoons baking powder
Salt to taste

Whip lard to the consistency of whipped cream. Mix with masa, add baking powder and salt, and beat until the mixture is so fluffy that when some of it is dropped into a cup of cold water the masa will float to the top. You may use prepared or creamed shortenings if you desire, but the lard improves the flavor. This is enough for approximately 25 medium-sized tamales.

Corn husks (may be purchased at a Mexican store) should be washed and soaked in warm water for at least 1 hour. When ready to use, drain well. Approximately 1½ pounds of husks will be required for the above amount of tamales.

In making the tamales, spread masa on husk (put on a spoonful of masa, then spread with back of spoon.) The filling goes on top of this masa. (See recipes for various fillings.) After putting on the filling, fold husk. To prevent leakage, spread another husk with more masa and wrap it around the first one which contains the filling. Be sure husks are not torn. Tie tamales at both ends with strips of husk or string, or fold over and tie at one end. Tamales should then be placed in a steamer, covered, and steamed over boiling water 45 minutes.

FILLINGS FOR TAMALES

Pork. Prepare 5 pounds of masa according to basic recipe given above. Cut 3 pounds of lean pork into cubes the size of large walnuts, cover with salted water, add 2 or 3 peeled whole cloves of garlic, cover, and simmer until tender. Remove garlic when meat is done. Then add the meat to this tamale sauce:

TAMALE SAUCE

In ½ cup oil brown 8 heaping tablespoons of flour. To this add 5 eight-ounce cans tomato sauce and 1 eight-oz. bottle of prepared red chile sauce which can be bought at any Mexican store—it already contains all the spices and seasonings. More chile sauce may be used if a stronger chile flavor is desired. Add meat. Let sauce cool completely before spreading over masa on tamales—makes it easier to handle, if you do! Tomato puree (made by forcing drained solid-pack tomatoes through a sieve) may be used instead of the sauce, although it will need additional seasoning. (Follow basic recipe for spreading filling on husks, and tying and steaming.)

Beef. Follow above recipe, using beef cubes instead of pork.

Chicken. Use fricasseed chicken, cut in pieces. Add to tamale sauce and let stand a short time. When cold, place a piece of chicken, dripping with the sauce, on the masa in each tamale, adding pickled string beans, pickled onions, pitted green or ripe olives, and pickled wax chiles as desired. Proceed as directed in basic recipe. (If preferred fresh, tomatoes or tomato puree or white sauce may be used instead of the tamale sauce given above. If fresh tomatoes are used, they should be skinned, chopped together with onion, and fried a few minutes in a little oil.)
Picadillo. In making picadillo tamales follow the basic recipe for the masa, and use picadillo for filling. Recipe for picadillo is given under Meats (page 55); add whole green or ripe olives, and strips of green chiles if desired.

Cheese Tamales. On the masa place a spoonful of refried beans, then pieces of Monterey cheese, then strips of green peeled chiles. Spread on masa on husks as directed in basic recipe.

Corn Tamales. Mix together 1 No. 2 can cream style corn, 2 cups corn meal, salt to taste, 6 tablespoons shortening, 2 teaspoons baking powder. Mix well. Take 2 tablespoons of this mixture and place in a clean husk, fold and tie. Fill the desired number of husks in same manner, place in steamer and cook over hot water for 30 to 40 minutes. For "Sweet Corn," use corn recipe, adding sugar and cinnamon to taste.

COCKTAIL TAMALES

Any of the tamales may be made in finger size, cutting down the cooking time to 20 minutes, and served hot as appetizers.

SWEET TAMALES WITH RAISINS

Use basic tamale recipe, adding sugar and cinnamon to the masa. Place heaping tablespoon of masa on each husk, then spread with any desired jam, or place raisins and blanched almonds in center. Anise flavoring may be used in place of cinnamon.

TAMAL EN CACEROLA
Corn Tamale Pie

1 large can tamales	2 eggs, beaten
1 can corn niblets	Salt and pepper to taste
1 can tomato sauce	2 tablespoons grated cheese

Break tamales into pieces, mix with corn, tomato sauce and beaten eggs. Add salt and pepper to taste. Pour into casserole. Sprinkle cheese over top and bake in a moderate oven (375°) 30 to 40 minutes, or until the center is firm. Garnish with ripe olives, if desired. Serves 4 to 6.

TAMAL FINGIDO
Mock Tamale

1 onion, minced	1½ pounds ground pork
⅓ cup oil	1 cup corn niblets
2½ cups tomato puree	2 eggs
Green peeled chile to taste	Salt and pepper to taste
1 cup corn meal	10 baby artichokes

Saute onion in oil; when brown add puree (canned solid-pack tomatoes which have been well mashed); add chile as desired. When this is well cooked, add corn meal, stirring constantly to keep from lumping, and cook 10 minutes. Remove from fire, add meat and corn; mix well. Beat eggs lightly and add to above mixture. Pour in buttered pan (square or loaf pan) and bake in a moderate oven (375°) 45 minutes to 1 hour. Turn out on platter, place cooked artichokes around it to look like little cactus plants. I like to add a tablespoon of vinegar, tablespoon of oil and a clove of garlic to the water in which the artichokes are cooked.

TAMALES DE ARROZ DULCES
Sweet Rice Tamales

1 pound rice	1 teaspoon cinnamon
1 cup butter	Pinch of salt
1 cup sugar	

Wash and dry rice in sun. Grind fine and mix with butter, beating until so fluffy that when some of it is dropped into a cup of cold water, the mixture will float to the top. Then add sugar and cinnamon and beat well. Use in place of the masa mixture on husks, filling center with jellies, jams, raisins, almonds or any other sweet filling. Steam as directed. Serve for dessert.

TAMALE NOTE

The average American family may not care to go to the trouble of looking up a Mexican store, or perhaps there may not be one in their town. In these cases, they can still have tamales which are tasty, following the recipe that I gave for Corn Tamales which calls for ingredients that may be obtained in any American store. Instead of husks, parchment paper may be used. Another variation for tamales is the tamale pie, which you can make to suit your individual taste, using half of the Corn Tamale recipe to cover the pie, and instead of baking, steam for 30 to 45 minutes. This gives the flavor of the original tamale, with a great deal less trouble. If sweet tamales are desired, follow the recipe for Sweet Corn Tamales, using the parchment paper instead of the husk.

MEXICAN METHOD OF MAKING MASA

3 pounds shelled corn	3 quarts cold water
3 ounces hydrated lime	

Place shelled corn in a pot, cover with cold water, and add the hydrated lime. Boil until corn begins to peel. (If Mexican corn is used, corn is not allowed to come completely to boil.) Remove from heat and cool. Rub corn between hands until skins separate from kernels; then rinse in cold water. This corn is called Nixtamal. The Nixtamal should be ground on a metate, or if not available, in a food chopper, using a very fine blade. The resulting dough is called Masa. This amount of corn makes 6 pounds of masa. Nixtamal and masa may be bought by the pound in Mexican stores.

TYPICAL MIDNIGHT SNACK
TAMALES (Steamed and Served Hot)   Chilled Beer
BUNUELOS EN FORMA DE FLOR (Flower-shaped Pastry)
Hot Chocolate or Coffee

Chapter Six

CARNES - Meats

METIENDO MUCHAS CUCHARAS, ECHAN A PERDER EL CALDO. (Too many cooks spoil the broth.)

CARNES—Meats

$\mathcal{M}$EXICANS *rarely serve meat plain-cooked as we do here in our country. Instead, they make it into all sorts of interesting combinations. This chapter gives recipes for some of the ones that are most practical from the standpoint of the northern cook. You will note that in these recipes I call frequently for tomato puree. As explained elsewhere, tomato puree is made by sieving drained, solid-pack canned tomatoes. You will note, too, that I call for various kinds of chiles, all of which are obtainable at Mexican stores. Canned green chiles, called for in many recipes, can be bought at almost any grocery or market. Incidentally, even though chiles are freely used, you will find that none of these dishes is extremely hot. Contrary to the idea all too common in the United States, good Mexican cooking is not necessarily hot. Hot sauces are usually served separately at table, to be added to the food as each individual desires.*

ALDILLA ADOBADA
Barbecued Flank Steak

1 large flank steak	2 tablespoons vinegar
2 cloves garlic	1 teaspoon oregano
Salt and pepper	1 can tomato sauce
3 tablespoons oil	

Cut flank steak into large pieces, mash garlic and rub all over meat. Season to taste. Add oil, vinegar and oregano (rubbed between palms of hands) and let stand at least 3 hours. About 20 minutes before serving time, pour tomato sauce over all and place under broiler, turning occasionally. If desired, cook longer. Serves 5 or 6.

ALDILLA RELLENA
Stuffed Flank Steak

1 large flank steak	¼ cup parsley, minced
1 clove garlic	½ cup celery, chopped fine
¼ cup oil	1 egg, beaten
3 chorizos (Mexican sausages)	Salt and pepper
6 green onions, chopped fine	1 cup broth (bouillon cubes may be used)

Place flank steak on a board and rub it with garlic and some of the oil. Remove skins from chorizos, crumble, add chopped onions, parsley, celery and beaten egg, and mix well. Spread this filling on top of steak and roll as you would a jelly roll; "pin" with toothpicks to hold meat together. Sprinkle with pepper, dredge with flour, and brown on all sides in oil, then add the broth. Cover and cook very slowly until meat is tender. Serves 6. This may be varied by using ¼ pound salami and ¼ cup grated cheese instead of the chorizos. Also tomato puree may be used instead of broth.

FILETE CON HONGOS
Filet Steak with Mushrooms

3 filet steaks	½ pound fresh mushrooms
3 tablespoons oil or butter	½ cup white wine
6 green onions, cut in rings	Salt and pepper
¼ cup parsley, minced	

Fry steaks quickly in oil or butter, remove to hot platter and keep hot. In remaining oil or butter fry onions, parsley and mushrooms which have been washed and cut into quarters. Add wine and salt and pepper and cook quickly until mushrooms are tender (about 5 minutes). Pour this over steaks. Decorate platter with slices of lemon and tomato. Serves 3.

CARNE MACHACADA CON HONGOS
Pounded Beefsteak with Mushrooms

2 lbs. top round steak	1 cup beef stock or bouillon
Flour	
Salt and pepper	1 medium-sized can of mushrooms
⅓ cup oil	
1 onion, minced	½ teaspoon paprika
¼ cup parsley, minced	

Pound flour, salt and pepper into steaks, cut into 3-inch strips and brown on both sides in hot oil. Remove steaks to a heavy kettle. In remaining oil fry onion and parsley about 5 minutes. Add beef stock and ½ cup liquid from mushrooms. Season with salt and pepper to taste; add paprika last. Pour this gravy over steaks, cover pot and cook very slowly for 1 hour, or until meat is tender. Add mushrooms 10 minutes before meat is done. Serves 4 to 6.

ARRECHERA ADOBADA
Barbecued Skirt Steak

1 skirt steak	1 teaspoon oregano
Salt and pepper	1 tablespoon vinegar
1 clove garlic, minced	3 tablespoons oil
	1 can tomato sauce

Cut steak into 2-inch squares and place in a shallow baking pan in which it will be broiled. Sprinkle with salt and pepper, minced garlic, and oregano (rubbed between the hands). Mix vinegar and oil, pour over all, and let stand for 2 hours. Add tomato sauce, then place pan under broiler and cook, turning occasionally, until meat is done. Serves 4.

I find skirt steak to be one of the best flavored, less expensive cuts of meat. It may be improved by letting it stand for several hours in a small amount of vinegar, oregano, garlic, salt and pepper. Often I let it soak in lemon juice, then season and broil.

CARNE DESHEBRADA
Shredded Skirt Steak, Mexican Style

1 large skirt steak	Fresh cilantro or
1 small onion, minced	1 teaspoon dried cilantro
¼ cup oil	(fresh is better)
2 large tomatoes, peeled	1 clove garlic
and chopped	Salt and pepper
1 bell pepper, chopped	

Cut steak into large pieces and broil medium rare. When cool, shred with a fork. In the oil fry onions until tender; add chopped tomato and bell pepper. Then add shredded meat and 1½ cups water; mash the dried cilantro and the garlic, add a little water and strain into the meat. (If fresh cilantro is used do not mash, but throw in whole leaves.) Salt and pepper to taste, cover, and simmer at least half an hour. This should be served in soup plates and eaten with soup spoons. Serves 4. If desired, this may be made drier by omitting some of the liquid. This meat may be mixed with eggs and scrambled, omitting 1 cup of water. Green peeled chiles may be added if desired.

CARNE EN JUGO DE NARANJA
Sliced Beef in Orange Juice

3 cloves garlic
½ teaspoon comino
½ teaspoon ground cloves
1 teaspoon salt
½ teaspoon pepper
3 pounds sirloin butt
1 bay leaf
1 large onion
2 cups orange juice

Mash garlic well, add comino, cloves, salt and pepper and make a paste out of all this. Make indentations in the beef with sharp pointed knife, and in each cut insert some of this paste until all is used. Simmer in slightly salted water, with bay leaf and onion, until tender. Cool, slice, place on deep platter and pour over all the orange juice. Let stand overnight or longer, turning meat occasionally. Garnish with round slices of fresh oranges. Serves 8.

CARNE TACHONADA
Fancy Spanish Pot Roast

¾ pound slice of smoked raw ham
3 cloves garlic, mashed to paste
5 pounds pot roast of beef
Salt and pepper
¼ cup oil
1 onion
½ a bell pepper
2 cups tomato puree

Cut ham into strips 1 inch long and ½ inch wide. Rub with garlic and insert into indentations which have been made with a sharp knife on the pot roast. Rub the roast well with salt and pepper and brown on all sides in hot oil. Mince onion and bell pepper, add tomato puree, pour over pot roast, cover, and cook slowly until tender—about 2½ hours. Serves 8 to 10.

ASADO CON PATAS DE PUERCO
Pot Roast with Pigs Feet

1½ lbs. beef in one piece
2 pigs feet
1 cup raw smoked ham, diced
2 onions
4 large carrots
1 pinch cloves
3 whole black peppers
½ cup vinegar
1 cup water
1 cup red wine
3 tablespoons oil
Salt to taste

Place beef in a sauce pan, add ham, pigs feet, onions, carrots, cloves, black pepper, vinegar and water. Cover pot with piece of brown paper, place the cover on top and tie so that steam will not escape.

Simmer for 2 hours. When 1 hour has elapsed, uncover, and add salt, then cover again and finish cooking. When meat is done take it out and brown in oil on all sides, then return to pot, add wine and cook a few minutes longer. Strain gravy, place all meats on platter and pour gravy over all. Serves 6.

I find in making pot roast, that a very nice variation is made by allowing the meat to stand for several hours in vinegar, oregano, garlic, salt and pepper to taste. After the meat is browned, if you will use white wine for liquid, instead of water, it will give you something so very different that the flavor will be outstanding.

ESTOFADO A LA ESPANOLA
Spanish Stew

4 tablespoons oil	½ cup tomato sauce
1½ pounds lean beef stew meat	3 tablespoons vinegar
	1 cup red table wine
1 medium-sized onion, minced	1 bay leaf
	1 teaspoon oregano
1 clove garlic, minced	Salt and pepper to taste

Place all ingredients cold in a pot which can be tightly covered, and let simmer from 1½ to 2 hours, or until meat is tender. If desired, carrots and potatoes may be added a half hour before the meat is done. Serves 4.

CARNE CON CHILE COLORADO
Beef or Pork in Red Chile Sauce

2 pounds beef or pork, cut in cubes	½ cup water in which chiles were soaked
8 chiles colorado (red chile)	2 tablespoons flour
	¼ cup oil
2 cloves garlic	Salt to taste
1 teaspoon oregano	Pinch (use sparingly)
1 cup water from meat	comino

Cook meat in 2 cups water with salt to taste for half an hour, and save water. While it cooks, soak chiles in warm water to cover, until soft, about 20 minutes; drain, saving the water. Remove seeds. Grind chiles, garlic, and oregano to consistency of paste; add 1 cup water from meat and ½ cup water in which chiles were soaked. Brown flour in oil; then gradually add the chile mixture; add comino and salt. Add to meat and broth and let simmer, covered, until tender, about 1 hour, Serves 4 to 6. This is very good with Mexican beans.

CHILE CON CARNE

Vary Carne con Chile Colorado by adding 1 can of kidney beans, and instead of the red chiles I call for in my recipe, it may be simplified by using either the powdered chile or the red chile sauce already prepared. A nice variation of this also may be made by using hominy instead of the kidney beans.

To cook a delicious Mexican steak, mix flour, salt, pepper and chile powder and pound this mixture into round steak. It may be served plain fried, or with chile sauce. I prefer the former.

ESTOFADO SONORENSE
Beef Stew, Sonora Style

2 pounds beef stew meat	1 tablespoon vinegar
1 large onion, minced	1 teaspoon oregano
2 cloves garlic, minced	Salt and pepper
1 bell pepper, diced	2 tablespoons flour
1 cup tomato puree	

Place meat in heavy pan, add minced onion, garlic, and bell pepper; pour tomato over all, then add vinegar, oregano (rubbed between palms of hands), salt and pepper, and last the flour sprinkled over all. Cook on top of stove, covered, approximately 1½ hours, or until tender. Do not use any shortening; the fat on the meat will be sufficient. Serves 6.

CARNE A LA VINAGRETA
Pickled Beef

2 pounds boiled beef	1 teaspoon prepared mustard
8 green onions	2 tablespoons finely minced
½ cup oil	parsley
¼ cup vinegar	Salt and pepper to taste

Slice beef and place in deep platter. Cut green onions into rings and place on top of meat. Mix well, oil, vinegar, mustard, parsley and salt and pepper. Pour over meat. Let stand at least 2 hours before serving. Serves 5 or 6.

ASADO A LA PLAZA
Mexican Country Style Roast

2 lbs. cooked boiling beef	1 cup boiled string beans
2 large potatoes, boiled in their jackets	(cut in small pieces)
	Shredded lettuce
3 large zucchini (sliced and boiled with 1 tablespoon vinegar added)	Salt and pepper

Cut beef into medium-sized cubes and fry until crisp in oil. Set aside. Peel potatoes, cut into medium-sized cubes, and fry. To serve, place a layer of meat, layer of potatoes, layer of cooked vegetables, and shredded lettuce, all of which have been seasoned to taste. Pour over all the following sauce: Mash well 2 cups solid-pack canned tomatoes (do not use tomato sauce). To this add 1 tablespoon vinegar, 2 tablespoons oil, 1½ teaspoons salt, 3 to 4 chile tepines (according to taste) mashed with 1 clove garlic. Add 1 teaspoon oregano (rubbed between palms of hands into the sauce). This sauce may be served hot or cold as desired. Serves 6.

PLATILLO FRIO A LA ESPANOLA
Cold Plate, Spanish Style

2 cups cubed cooked beef	1 tablespoon minced parsley
1 cup cubed boiled ham	4 tablespoons olive oil
1 can pimientos, diced	2 tablespoons vinegar
1 large onion, cut in rings	Salt and pepper

Mix beef, ham and pimientos; add onion rings, parsley, oil, vinegar, and salt and pepper to taste. Serve cold on platter, sprinkling with a little paprika. Serves 4.

NIDO DE PAPA Y CARNE
Mexican Meat Casserole Dish

2 cups mashed potatoes	1 cup tomato puree
1 egg yolk, beaten	1½ lbs. boiled beef, cubed
1 tablespoon chopped onion	½ pound raw ham, cubed
1 tablespoon minced parsley	2 tablespoons butter
	Salt and pepper
2 tablespoons oil	

Prepare mashed potatoes in the usual way, but add the egg yolks and beat well. Fry onion and parsley in oil; add tomato puree and the cubed beef and ham. Season well. In a buttered casserole put a layer of mashed potatoes, then one of meat in sauce; repeat, having top layer potatoes. Dot with butter and bake for half an hour in a moderately hot oven (375°). Serves 6,

CHULETAS
Ground Beef Steaks

1½ pounds ground beef	3 pieces bread, soaked in water
1 onion, grated	½ teaspoon nutmeg
1 clove garlic, mashed	Salt and pepper

Place meat in bowl, add grated onion, garlic paste and soaked bread, nutmeg, salt and pepper to taste. Mix thoroughly. Pat into 12 strips about 6 inches long, and, with a fork, make ridges lengthwise on the strips. Fry lightly on both sides. In Mexico these steaks are made on the metate (which is a Mexican grindstone) and the ridges are made automatically. Not having a metate, we are doing the next best thing! Chuletas may be served with the following sauce: In 3 tablespoons oil fry 1 large onion (either minced or cut in rings); add 1½ cups well-mashed solid-pack canned tomatoes and ½ cup water from green olives. Season to taste with salt and pepper. Add olives or pickled waxed peppers. Serves 6.

ALBONDIGAS CON CHILE COLORADO
Meat Balls with Red Chile Sauce

¾ pound ground beef	1½ teaspoons salt
¾ pound ground pork	¼ teaspoon pepper
2 slices bread, soaked in hot milk and drained	2 tablespoons oil
1 egg, beaten	1 8-oz. bottle red chile sauce (bought at Mexican store)

Mix thoroughly the meat, bread, egg, and salt and pepper, and make into meat balls the size of walnuts. Heat oil, add chile sauce and sufficient water or broth to suit your taste; add meat balls to this gravy and cook, covered, for 45 minutes. Will serve 6.

ALBONDIGAS EN SALSA DE ALMENDRA
Meat Balls in Almond Sauce

2 tablespoons minced onion	3 slices bread
3 tablespoons oil	¾ pound ground beef
¼ cup strained tomato puree	¾ pound ground pork
1½ cups water	1 egg, beaten
½ cup almonds	1½ teaspoons salt
1 clove garlic, peeled	¼ teaspoon pepper

Fry onion in 1 tablespoon of the oil; add tomato puree and water. Season to taste and cook slowly. In remaining oil fry the almonds, garlic and 1 slice of bread until brown. When cold, grind to consistency of paste. Dilute with a little water and strain into the tomato sauce.

Prepare meat in the following way: Soak 2 slices of bread in a little hot milk, drain and add, with the egg, to the meat; add salt and pepper and mix thoroughly. Roll into small balls and add to the boiling sauce, cover well, and cook for half an hour. If desired, cubed potatoes may be added and cooked with the balls. Serves 6 to 8.

In making Albondigas a different flavor may be obtained by adding chile powder to the meats. Wedges of hard-cooked eggs or spoonfuls of grated carrot may be inserted in the meat balls before cooking.

ALBONDIGONES CON ALCAPARRAS
Large Meat Balls with Capers

2 pounds ground pork
2 slices bread soaked in hot milk and drained
4 eggs
Salt and pepper
1 bottle capers
2 tablespoons flour
2 tablespoons minced onion
1 clove garlic, minced
½ cup oil
3 to 4 tablespoons chile powder

Mix meat, bread, 1 beaten egg and salt and pepper. Shape into balls the size of a large walnut and insert 4 capers in each ball. Beat 3 egg whites stiff but not dry; beat yolks, fold into whites and add 2 tablespoons flour. Drop meat balls into batter, coating them all over, then fry. Remove to absorbent paper to drain. (They are not thoroughly cooked as yet, so do not taste them; pork must always be very well done.) Make a thin sauce as follows: fry onion and garlic in the oil; add water sufficient to cover meat balls. Mix chile powder with a little cold water and add also additional capers as desired. When sauce is boiling, add meat balls, and simmer, covered, for 45 minutes. Serves 8 to 12.

PICADILLO
Mexican Hash

1 medium-sized onion, minced
1 clove garlic, minced
4 tablespoons oil
2 fresh tomatoes, peeled
2 cups chopped cooked beef
½ cup soup stock
¼ cup raisins
1 teaspoon vinegar
1 pinch cloves
1 small pinch comino
Salt and pepper

Fry onion and garlic in oil about 5 minutes. Add chopped tomatoes. Add meat, stirring these ingredients together well. Add soup stock and remaining ingredients, and simmer about half an hour. Serves 4. Makes a very good stuffing for tamales or tacos.

TORTA DE CARNE RELLENA
Baked Stuffed Meat Loaf

2 pounds ground beef	¼ cup oil
2 slices bread, soaked in milk	2 fresh tomatoes, peeled
	1 cup diced cooked carrots
2 eggs.	1 cup cooked peas
2 teaspoons salt	½ cup cooked string beans,
¼ teaspoon pepper, or more	cut small
2 tablespoons minced onion	1 cup beef stock

Mix well meat, bread (soaked in hot milk and drained), 1 egg and salt and pepper to taste. Pat out meat on waxed paper with the hand, as you do biscuits. Spread the following filling on top of the meat and roll as you would a jelly roll. Be sure that all the vegetables are inside the roll. Filling: Fry onion in half the oil until just tender but not browned. Add chopped tomato, cook for a few minutes, then add other vegetables. Season to taste. When cold, add the remaining egg, beaten, and mix well. Spread on meat and roll as described. Put into a baking pan, greased with rest of oil, and bake, uncovered, in a moderately hot oven (375°) until brown, approximately 20 minutes. Sprinkle a little flour over the top, and add 1 cup of stock. Cover and cook for 1 hour, lowering temperature to 350°. Serves 8.

TORTA DE CARNE RELLENA (HERVIDA)
Stuffed Meat Loaf, Boiled

Follow the recipe for stuffed meat loaf, but instead of baking, boil in the following manner: Fill large pan about ¾ full of water, add salt, 1 large onion, a few whole black peppers, 2 cloves garlic, and a bay leaf. Heat to boiling, tie meat loaf in cheese cloth. Submerge bag in boiling liquid and simmer for 1 hour. This may be served sliced, hot or cold, as desired.

TORTA DE CARNE MEXICANA
Mexican Meat Loaf

2 pounds ground raw beef (or leftover cooked meat)	1 egg, beaten
1 onion, minced	2 tomatoes, peeled and chopped
2 slices stale bread (or equivalent in bread crumbs)	1 cup red chile sauce (bought at Mexican store)
Salt	½ cup tomato juice

Chop meat and add onion, together with bread and salt to taste. Mix thoroughly with beaten egg, tomatoes, and chile sauce. Form into loaf. Heat 4 tablespoons fat in a small roaster, place loaf in pan, bake uncovered in a moderately hot oven (400°) until brown all over, then add tomato juice and enough hot water to half cover the meat. Cover and bake for 1 hour in a moderate oven (350°). Serves 6.

PIERNA DE TERNERA A LA ESPANOLA
Leg of Veal, Spanish Style

4 tablespoons oil
1 small leg of veal, boned
   and rolled
½ pound bacon, cut in cubes
1 large onion, minced
2 large carrots, chopped

2 cups boiling water
1 cup dry Sherry wine
1 bay leaf
Pinch of thyme
Salt and pepper

Heat oil and in it brown rolled leg of veal. Add cubed bacon, minced onion and carrots and fry for a few minutes, then add boiling water, Sherry, and herbs. Season to taste, cover tightly and cook until tender.

TERNERA EN RAJAS A LA ESPANOLA
Veal Strips, Spanish Style

2 large veal steaks
   (about 1½ pounds)
Juice of 2 lemons
Salt and pepper
Bacon drippings

1 cup fine bread crumbs
¼ cup minced parsley
¼ cup grated cheese
½ cup oil

Cut veal into small strips, soak for a few minutes in lemon juice, then season with salt and pepper; roll them in melted bacon fat and then in the bread crumbs which have been mixed with the parsley and cheese. Fry in oil until brown. Place in buttered casserole, dot with butter, sprinkle about 1 tablespoon water over them, and bake for half an hour in a moderate oven (350°) for half an hour. Serves 4.

TERNERA CON ALCACHOFA
Veal with Artichoke

Salt, pepper and flour about 2 pounds of veal round which has been cut into long strips. Brown in a little oil in a heavy saucepan. Add 1 onion, minced, and brown lightly. Add ⅓ cup minced parsley. Slice about a dozen small artichokes into rings, removing tough parts as they are being cut. Add artichokes to veal. Dissolve 1 or 2 bouillon cubes in 1 cup water or stock, add 1 teaspoon paprika. Pour this mixture over veal and artichokes, salt and pepper to taste, cover, and cook slowly about 45 minutes. Serves 6 to 8.

PIERNA DE CARNERO ADOBADA
Barbecued Leg of Lamb

2 cloves garlic	2 tablespoons vinegar
1 tablespoon oregano	3 tablespoons oil
1 pinch comino (optional)	Salt and pepper
1 leg lamb	

Mash garlic, oregano and comino into a paste. Make indentations with a sharp pointed knife in the leg of lamb and fill with the paste. Season, pour vinegar and oil over meat and let stand over night. Roast as you would an ordinary leg of lamb, uncovered, allowing 30 minutes per pound. The following Mexican cold sauce may be served with the lamb if desired.

2 cups tomato puree	2 tablespoons oil
2 tablespoons finely minced onions	1 teaspoon oregano (rubbed between palms of hands)
1 tablespoon vinegar	Salt and pepper

Mix ingredients well, and add chopped peeled green chiles in the amount desired.

COSTILLAS DE CARNERO RELLENAS
Stuffed Lamb Chops

6 French lamb chops	2 cups milk
½ cup butter or shortening	2 or 3 eggs, well beaten
2 tablespoons minced onion	Cracker meal or finely grated
4 slices boiled ham, minced	bread crumbs
8 tablespoons flour	1 cup oil

Have French lamb chops scraped to the top by butcher, shaping the meat into a sort of nest or cup. Pound the chops, sprinkle with salt and pepper, and place on a pan. Cook minced onion gently in butter (do not allow butter to brown), add minced ham, then flour and blend well. Gradually stir in cold milk, and cook, stirring constantly, until very thick. Season with salt and pepper. While hot, pour this sauce over each lamb chop and let cool. When cold, press into the chops, then dip carefully into the beaten egg, then into bread crumbs; repeat this dipping. Brown on both sides in hot oil, then remove to a baking pan that can be covered. Be sure stuffing is face up. About 45 minutes before serving time, sprinkle 1 or 2 tablespoons water over chops and bake in a moderately slow oven (325°). Decorate bone of each chop with paper frills. Serves 6.

COSTILLAS DE CARNERO CON CHICHAROS
Lamb Chops with Peas, Mexican Style

6 large lamb chops	2 fresh large tomatoes,
1 clove garlic, mashed	peeled
Salt and pepper to taste	½ cup water
½ cup oil	1 teaspoon oregano
1 onion, minced	8 new red potatoes
1 small green bell pepper,	1 cup fresh peas
chopped	

Rub chops with mashed garlic, sprinkle with salt and pepper, then brown on both sides in a little oil in a skillet; remove to another pan. In same skillet fry onion and green pepper; add chopped tomatoes and water, then rub oregano between palms of hands into sauce. Season with salt and pepper to taste. Add chops and cook for ½ hour, well covered, then add potatoes which have been scraped and cut into quarters; then add peas and cook for another 20 minutes. Best results are obtained if this dish is cooked in a very heavy pot so that it will be practically steamed. Serves 6.

CARNERO A LA ESPANOLA
Lamb with Beans, Spanish Style

2 cups uncooked white navy
    beans
½ pound bacon, in one piece
2 onions, chopped
3 tablespoons oil
1 pound lamb, cut in large
    cubes

1 cup tomato puree
1 tablespoon flour
Salt and pepper
1 bay leaf
2 balls chorizo Espanol
    (Spanish sausage)

Soak beans overnight, drain, cover with water and cook with bacon until tender. While they are cooking, fry onions in oil until soft, add lamb cubes and brown on all sides, then add tomato puree and 2 cups boiling water. Mix flour with a little cold water and stir into the above; add salt and pepper, bay leaf, and Spanish sausage cut in slices. Cook, covered, for 1 hour. Butter a casserole and place in it a layer of beans, then a layer of cooked lamb mixture; repeat this procedure, having last layer beans. Cut cooked bacon into strips and lay on top of beans. Bake in a moderately hot oven (375°) for half an hour. Serves 8.

COSTILLAS DE PUERCO EN ADOBADO
Pork Chops in Chile Sauce

8 pork chops
2 cloves garlic
Salt and pepper

1 tablespoon oregano
¼ cup vinegar
3 tablespoons (or more)
    chile powder

Mash garlic well and rub over pork chops; salt and pepper them and sprinkle with oregano which has been rubbed between palms of hands; then sprinkle vinegar over chops. Dissolve chile powder in sufficient water to cover chops and add. Let stand overnight in this chile sauce. When ready to use, bake in the sauce, in a moderately hot oven (375°) turning a couple of times, until chops are done — about 45 minutes. Serves 8.

COSTILLAS DE PUERCO EN TOMATE
Pork Chops in Tomato Sauce

6 large loin pork chops
2 tablespoons oil
Salt and pepper

2 cups tomato puree
1 clove garlic
1 can pimientos, cut in strips

Salt and pepper chops and brown on both sides in oil. Add tomato puree. Mash garlic with a little water and strain into the sauce. Salt and pepper to taste. Add pimientos, cover, and cook for 30 minutes. Serves 6.

COSTILLAS DE PUERCO EN SALSA DE CACAHUATE
Pork Chops in Peanut Butter Sauce

6 large pork chops
   ½ inch thick
Salt and pepper
Flour

1 onion, minced
½ cup peanut butter
2 cups milk

Salt and pepper the chops, roll in flour, fry until brown, then place in a casserole. In the same skillet fry the minced onion until soft, then add milk and peanut butter, stirring until smooth; pour over chops and bake for 45 minutes in a moderately hot oven (375°). This served with white rice makes a delicious combination.

COSTILLAS DE PUERCO EMPANIZADAS A LA ESPANOLA
Breaded Pork Chops, Spanish Style

6 pork chops
1 cup finely grated bread
   crumbs
1 clove garlic, minced

2 tablespoons minced parsley
2 tablespoons oil
Salt and pepper
1 can pimientos

Make a paste of the bread crumbs, garlic, parsley, salt and pepper, and oil. Then pound this paste into the pork chops; fry slowly until brown and well done. Serve on hot platter with pimientos which have been sauted in oil. Serves 6. Lamb chops may be used instead of pork if desired.

LOMO DE PUERCO
Loin of Pork, Mexican Style

2 pounds lean pork loin
2 cloves garlic
Black pepper (pepper
   corns)
6 chiles colorado (red
   chiles)

1 teaspoon oregano
Pinch of comino
3 tablespoons oil
Salt

Boil pork in salted water to which has been added 1 clove garlic and whole black pepper (pepper corns). Slice, add to it the following sauce: Wash chiles, remove seeds, and soak pods in warm water until tender, about 20 minutes. Grind to the consistency of paste the chiles, remaining clove of garlic, oregano and comino. Add 2 cups of the liquid in which the pork was cooked; mix with the paste and strain. Heat oil, add the sauce, adding salt and pepper to taste. Lastly add sliced meat and cook about 15 minutes, until well seasoned. Serve garnished with rings of onions which have been soaked in salt water and vinegar. Serves 4.

CARNE DE PUERCO CON CHILE VERDE
Pork with Green Chile Sauce

2 pounds lean pork	1 large minced onion
Water to cover	1 teaspoon cilantro
2 cloves garlic	1½ cups tomato puree
1 teaspoon salt	2 green peeled chiles, minced
½ teaspoon pepper	(more if you like it hot)

Cut meat into large cubes and cook until partly tender with water, 1 clove garlic, salt and pepper. While it cooks make the following sauce: Fry onion until brown in 2 tablespoons oil; add tomato puree. Mash remaining clove garlic and cilantro to a paste; add about ½ cup of the water in which pork was cooked, strain into sauce; add the chopped chiles. Drain the meat, add hot to the sauce, and let simmer until tender, approximately half an hour. Serves 4 or 5.

When roasting pork, I find that a very nice variation is to blend half a cup of peanut butter with 2 cups milk, and baste the roast with this mixture after removing drippings. This makes a delicious gravy, and no additional thickening is needed.

WAYS WITH SPARE RIBS

We have a Mexican recipe called Pozole which contains pig's head (boiled and the meat separated), chile sauce and hominy. Personally I prefer to make it by using pork spare ribs and cubed pork meat, instead of the pig's head, as I find the head too greasy. My version is made in the following manner: Have pork spare ribs cut into pieces, mix with an equal amount of cubed pork and cook in water to cover, with minced onion, minced garlic, salt and pepper to taste. When this is partly cooked, dissolve in some of the water from the meat, enough chile powder or chile sauce to suit your taste, add to pork and allow to cook until tender. Add canned hominy, including the liquid and cook a little longer. This may be served in soup plates with green minced onions over the top, and eaten with a spoon as you would eat soup. This is a wonderful dish for a large party.

PUCHERO
Spanish Boiled Dinner

1 fricassee chicken, cut in pieces
6 quarts water
Salt and pepper
2 cups garbanzos (soak over-
    night in salted water)
6 Spanish sausages
½ pound salt pork
2 pounds shoulder of lamb
¾ pound ground beef

¾ pound ground pork
2 eggs, beaten
½ cup grated bread crumbs
2 tablespoons flour
6 potatoes, peeled and
    quartered
1 bunch carrots, cut in
    strips
1 medium sized cabbage,
    cut in wedges

Wash chicken, cover with the cold water, add salt and pepper, and boil 10 minutes, then turn down heat and let simmer for 30 minutes. Skim. Add drained soaked garbanzos, sausages, salt pork, and shoulder of lamb. Then add the beef and pork which have been prepared as follows: add eggs, bread crumbs, flour, salt and pepper to beef and pork, and shape into a large ball. Place this on top of the chicken, etc., and cook until garbanzos are done, or approximately 1 hour longer. The vegetables should be added during the last 30 minutes. This is a complete meal in itself, and is perfect for family gatherings, as it will serve 10 or 12.

PLATANOS RELLENOS CON SALCHICHAS
Sausage Baked in Bananas

6 green-tipped bananas   12 small link sausages
(unpeeled)

Slit each banana lengthwise from tip to tip to make a pocket, being careful not to cut through the skin on the underside. Place 2 link sausages in the opening of each banana. Arrange bananas in baking dish, slit side up, and bake in moderately hot oven (375°) 15 to 20 minutes, or until sausages are well done. Serves 6.

CHORIZO CON HUEVOS
Mexican Sausages with Eggs

1 chorizo (Mexican sau-
    sage) for each person
    served

1 tablespoon oil for each
    chorizo
2 eggs for each chorizo

Remove skins from chorizos, crumble into hot oil and fry. Beat eggs, add to chorizo. Stir with a fork as you would scrambled eggs. If desired, minced onion may be added before adding eggs.

IF YOU CAN'T BUY CHORIZO

Many Mexican dishes contain chorizo. Realizing that it may not be obtainable in all parts of the country, I am giving a simple recipe which can be made in any home as follows: Grind 1 pound pork, not too fine, or if preferred, chop it. To this add 1 teaspoon salt, 1 tablespoon chile powder; mash 1 large clove of garlic very thoroughly with 2 tablespoons vinegar, add to the meat and mix well. The difference between this chorizo and the Mexican chorizo is that in the latter the spices are added individually, while in the above recipe they are all contained in the chile powder. Chorizo as bought is in casings; this is not necessary, as the chorizo can be packed in a crock or glass jar and it will keep, in a cool place, for several weeks.

TRIPA CON SALSA DE ALMENDRA
Tripe with Almond Sauce

2 pounds tripe	1 sprig parsley
2 thin slices French bread	½ an onion
¼ cup oil	1½ cups beef stock
½ cup almonds	Salt and pepper
1 clove garlic, peeled	

Wash and cut tripe into long strips like macaroni. Simmer in 1 quart of salted water for 1 hour. While it simmers, make the following sauce: Fry French bread in part of oil until brown; remove from pan. Fry almonds and whole clove garlic and remove from pan. Grind bread, garlic, almonds, parsley and onion to consistency of paste. Mix beef stock with paste. Season with salt and pepper. Add this mixture to remaining hot oil, add drained tripe, and cook, uncovered, until tender. Serves 4 to 6.

TRIPA A LA ESPANOLA
Spanish Tripe

3 pounds tripe	½ cup tomato sauce
1 large onion, minced	1 bay leaf
2 cloves garlic, minced	1 teaspoon oregano
⅓ cup oil	2 chile tepines (if not avail-
2½ cups tomato puree	able, add Tabasco sauce)
	Salt and pepper

Wash and cut tripe into long strips like macaroni. Simmer in 1 quart salted water for 1 hour. While it cooks, make the following sauce: Fry minced onion and garlic in oil about 5 minutes; add rest of ingredients and cook, covered, half an hour. Then add drained tripe and cook until tender, uncovered. If desired, 1 can of pimientos cut in strips may be added at the last. Serves 8 to 10. No definite time can be given for this: sometimes tripe will cook tender very quickly, while at other times an hour or more will be required, depending upon the treatment of the tripe before it is bought.

RINONES EN VINO BLANCO
Kidneys in White Wine

6 lamb kidneys	4 tablespoons oil
1 teaspoon vinegar	2 tablespoons minced
1 clove garlic, minced	parsley
6 green onions, minced	¾ cup white wine

Remove skins from kidneys and cut into small pieces. Wash and let stand in cold water with a teaspoon of vinegar added for half an hour. Wash again and drain thoroughly. Fry minced garlic and onion in the oil until soft; add parsley and kidneys; season, cover tightly, and simmer about 15 minutes; when almost done, add the white wine. Serves 3.

ESTOFADO DE CONEJO A LA ESPANOLA
Rabbit Stew, Spanish Style

1 rabbit, cleaned and cut in pieces	1 bay leaf
1 clove garlic, whole	¼ cup oil
1 onion, minced	1 cup white table wine
2 fresh tomatoes, peeled	1 tablespoon vinegar
	Salt and pepper

Salt and pepper pieces of rabbit, roll in flour, and fry in plenty of oil, with clove of garlic in the oil. When rabbit is well browned, remove and discard garlic; transfer rabbit to a pan that can be well covered and add the onion, chopped tomatoes, bay leaf, oil, wine, and vinegar. Salt and pepper to taste, cover tightly and cook on low heat for 1 hour or until tender. Serves 4 to 6.

TYPICAL MEALS

●

MEXICAN BREAKFAST
JUGO DE TORONJA HELADA (Chilled Grapefruit Juice)
CHORIZO CON HUEVOS (Mexican Sausage with Eggs)
FRIJOLES REFRITOS (Refried Beans)
TORTILLAS CALIENTES (Hot Tortillas)
Coffee or Chocolate
Yes, refried beans are served for breakfast!

●

MEXICAN LUNCH
CALDO DE GALLINA (Clear Chicken Broth)
CHALUPAS (Corn Patties)
FRIJOLES REFRITOS (Refried Beans)
NATILLA (Custard with Caramel Sauce)   Coffee

●

DINNER
SOPA DE BOLITAS DE LECHE (Soup with Custard Balls)
ENSALADA DE AGUACATE RELLENO
(Stuffed Avocado Salad)
ALDILLA RELLENA (Stuffed Flank Steak)
COLACHE (Summer Squash)
EMPANADAS (Small Filled Cookies)   Chilled Fruit
Coffee

MERIENDA
Equivalent to an American Tea
This is an afternoon custom in Mexico when Mexican chocolate is
served in pretty *jarros* (Mexican earthen pots) and stirred with a
molinillo (a long wooden beater with a ball and rings on the end) until
the chocolate is foamy. This is accompanied by dainty sweet tamales,
or Mexican bread or cookies. Mexican chocolate may be obtained at
Mexican stores. It is marked into quarters, each quarter making 1 cup
of chocolate. Mexican chocolate is strongly flavored with cinnamon.

Chapter Seven
POLLOS - Chicken

MAS CERCA ESTAN LOS DIENTES QUE LOS PARIENTES. (Our teeth are closer to us than our relatives.)

POLLOS—Chicken

*F*owl is an *all-time favorite in Mexico. Here, again, sauces and
seasonings play a big part, and rare is the bird that goes to the
table without a fancy dressing. These recipes adapt themselves
beautifully to North-of-the-Border menus and appetites. Such
dishes as Arroz a la Valenciana, Arroz con Pollo, and the like,
make excellent buffet supper dishes . . . Please note that Mexican
chicken soup is different in that the chicken is left in large pieces,
and not cut up into little bits as we do in this country. This would
be excellent with a green salad for Sunday night supper.*

ALBONDIGAS DE GALLINA
Chicken Balls, Mexican Style

3 cups chopped cooked chicken	⅛ teaspoon cloves
2 cloves garlic	2 quarts boiling salted water
2 slices bread, soaked and drained	¼ cup butter
2 tomatoes, peeled	¾ cup almonds, blanched and ground very fine
1 egg	Salt and pepper

Grind chicken, garlic, bread and tomatoes. To this add the egg and
cloves. Mix these ingredients well and form into balls the size of a
walnut. To the boiling salted water add the butter. Drop in the chicken
balls and allow to cook about 20 minutes. Remove chicken balls with
skimmer. Allow broth to boil down about one-third and thicken with
ground almonds. Return chicken balls to broth and heat through.
When ready to serve, minced green chiles or minced green pepper may
be added. Serves 4 or 5.

POLLO EN MOLE VERDE
Chicken in Green Mole Sauce

1 fricassee chicken, cut in pieces
2 tablespoons pumpkin seeds
4 long green chiles
¾ cup chopped parsley
3 cups chicken broth
¼ cup oil
Salt and pepper

Cook chicken until tender, using just enough water to cover chicken, in order to make a strong broth. While chicken cooks, make the sauce. Toast pumpkin seeds until brown. Place chiles under the broiler, turning until skin blisters, place in paper bag for 15 minutes, then remove skin and seeds. Grind pumpkin seeds, chiles and parsley very fine, put through the grinder twice if necessary. Rinse the grinder with some of the hot chicken broth, then strain. Add the strained mixture and remaining broth to the hot oil, heat thoroughly, then add the chicken and simmer for 15 minutes. Serves 6.

POLLO CON ARROZ
Chicken with Rice

1 frying chicken
½ cup oil
1 cup rice, uncooked
½ an onion, chopped
1 clove garlic, minced
¼ cup tomato puree
2½ cups boiling water
Salt and pepper

Cut chicken in pieces and fry in oil until a delicate brown. Remove from pan. Add the unwashed, uncooked rice to the oil in the pan and fry until golden, stirring frequently. Add onion, garlic, tomato puree and boiling water. Season with salt and pepper. Add the browned chicken, and let simmer, covered, for 30 minutes. Do not remove cover. It must steam thoroughly. Serves 4 to 6.

POLLO CON HONGOS
Chicken with Mushrooms

2 frying chickens, cut into pieces
½ cup oil
8 green onions, minced
2 cloves garlic, minced
¼ cup minced parsley
1 cup white table wine
½ pound mushrooms
Salt and pepper to taste

Salt and pepper pieces of chicken and brown well in hot oil. Add minced onions, garlic and parsley and cook, stirring, for a few minutes; then add the white wine. Cover and simmer until the chicken is tender. The mushrooms, which have been washed and sliced, should be added about 15 minutes before serving. Season to taste. Serves 4 to 6.

POLLO A LA PLAZA
Mexican Country-Style Chicken

1 fricassee chicken, cut in pieces

2 large potatoes, boiled in jackets

1 cup cooked string beans, cut in small pieces

3 large zucchini (sliced and boiled with 1 tablespoon vinegar added)

Shredded lettuce

Salt and pepper

Cook the chicken in hot water seasoned with salt, pepper, and chopped celery, carrots, onion and parsley. When tender, remove from broth, dry well, and fry in oil or other fat until brown. Set aside. Remove skins from potatoes, cut into medium-sized cubes, and fry. To serve, place a layer of fried chicken, a layer of potatoes, a layer of zucchini and beans and shredded lettuce—all of which have been seasoned to taste. Pour over all the following sauce: Mash well 2 cups pureed tomato. To this add 1 tablespoon vinegar, 2 tablespoons oil, 1½ teaspoons salt, 3 or 4 chile tepines, mashed with 1 clove garlic, then add 1 teaspoon oregano (rubbed between palms of hands into the sauce). Sauce may be served hot or cold.

GALLINA EN SALSA DE ACEITUNAS
Chicken with Olive Sauce

1 fricassee chicken, cut in pieces

1 small bell pepper, minced

1 onion

1 clove garlic

1 teaspoon oregano

1 inch stick cinnamon

1 teaspoon cilantro (sometimes known as culantro or coriander)

1 doz. green olives, sliced

1 slice bread, soaked in water

1 quart chicken broth

½ cup tomato puree

2 tablespoons flour

⅓ cup oil

2 dozen whole green olives

¼ cup seedless raisins (optional)

Salt and pepper

Pinch comino (use sparingly)

1 teaspoon vinegar

Simmer chicken in 3 quarts water, with seasoning to taste, until very tender. Grind very fine green pepper, onion, garlic, oregano, cinnamon, culantro, 12 green olives, and soaked break. Add to this 1 cup of chicken broth and tomato puree and force through a strainer. Brown the flour in the hot oil; gradually stir in the cold chicken broth and finally the strained mixture. Add the cooked chicken, remaining 12 whole olives, and raisins. Season to taste. Lastly add the comino and vinegar. Cook for 30 minutes longer, covered. If desired, pickled wax peppers may be added whole to the above sauce.

PICHON EN ARROZ A LA ESPANOLA
Pigeon with Rice, Spanish Style

1 young pigeon	1 pound shrimps
1 medium onion	Meat of 1 crab
⅓ cup oil	2 cups boiling water
1 cup rice	Salt and pepper
½ cup tomato puree	¼ cup minced parsley
2 pounds clams in the shell	

Clean and cut up pigeon. Boil clams in a little salted water until shells open; remove from shell; clean shrimps. Fry onion well in oil, add pigeon and rice and allow to cook a few minutes, stirring frequently. Add tomato puree and clams, shrimps and crab meat; then add boiling water. Season with salt and pepper to taste, and add parsley last. Cook, covered, about 30 minutes. If possible, serve from dish in which it was cooked. If an earthenware dish is used, it will improve the flavor. This will serve 8 persons.

POLLOS BORRACHOS
Chicken Roasters, Drunkard Style

2 3-pound roasting chickens, cut in pieces	1 inch stick of cinnamon
4 tablespoons oil	¼ teaspoon cloves
3 onions, cut in rings	1 bay leaf
⅓ cup parsley	2 tablespoons vinegar
2 tablespoons sesame seed	¼ cup dry Sherry wine
4 whole black peppers	16 green olives
	4 green peeled chiles (or less)
	Salt

Put 2 tablespoons oil in bottom of Dutch oven or kettle in which chicken is to be cooked. Put in onion rings, parsley, sesame seed, whole black peppers, cinnamon stick, cloves and bay leaf. Now add chicken. Pour over the top of chickens the remaining oil, vinegar, Sherry; add whole olives and green peeled chiles, cut in strips. Salt to taste. Cover pot tightly and simmer for 1 hour, occasionally turning chicken lightly. Serves 8.

POLLO CON CASTANAS A LA ESPANOLA
Chicken with Chestnuts, Spanish Style

1 medium-sized roasting chicken, cut in pieces
Juice of 1 lemon
Salt and pepper
6 tablespoons oil
1 onion, minced
½ cup cubed raw smoked ham
1 cup chicken broth
½ cup dry Sherry wine
12 chestnuts, shelled and blanched
½ cup blanched almonds

Wash chicken and pour lemon juice over it; sprinkle with salt and pepper, then brown in the oil. Add onion, ham, broth and Sherry wine, cover and allow to cook slowly. While it cooks, shell and blanch chestnuts and toast together with almonds, then grind to consistency of paste. When chicken is almost done, add the paste of chestnuts and almonds, and continue cooking until it is tender. Serves 4. (To shell and blanch chestnuts easily, cut a slit in shell of each nut, place in a heavy frying pan with just enough oil to coat the shells and heat about 10 minutes, shaking pan frequently, or heat in oven about 20 minutes. When cool enough to handle, remove shells and skins with a sharp knife.)

ARROZ A LA VALENCIANA
Chicken with Rice, Valencia Style

1 roasting chicken, cut in pieces
½ pound pork sausages
1 rack pork spare ribs (about 2 pounds) cut into small pieces
1 large onion, minced
2 cloves garlic, minced
½ cup tomato puree
1 can wet-pack shrimps
6 cups water
1 cup peas
1 cup string beans
1 can pimientos
¼ cup chopped parsley
1 teaspoon pimenton (sweet paprika)
3 or 4 strands saffron (or more)
2 cups rice

In a heavy wide pan fry first the pieces of chicken, then the sausages, then the spareribs, separately in hot oil, seasoning while frying. Remove each from pan when browned. To oil in pan add minced onion and garlic and brown lightly. Put in chicken, sausages and spareribs, add tomato puree and water. Use liquid from canned shrimps for part of water. Cover and let cook 15 minutes. Add all remaining ingredients except saffron and rice. While this mixture cooks, brown the saffron in a dry skillet; this makes it crisp and easily broken. Add saffron and rice, cover, and cook 30 minutes over low heat. Serve at once on platter; or better yet, wrap the pot in fluted yellow and red crepe paper and take to the table. Serves 12.

POLLO EN TOMATE CON HONGOS
Chicken in Tomato Sauce with Mushrooms

2 frying chickens, cut in
pieces
½ cup oil
6 green onions, whole
2 cloves garlic, minced
Salt and pepper to taste

1½ cans tomato sauce
1 cup chicken broth or
water
1 medium sized can mush-
rooms
½ cup mushroom liquid

Season pieces of chicken with salt and pepper and fry in oil until
brown. Add the minced garlic and the whole onions. Stir until well
mixed. Add the tomato sauce, chicken broth and mushroom liquid.
Add more salt and pepper, if necessary. Cook, tightly covered, until
done—about 30 minutes; add the mushrooms 5 minutes before serving. Serves 4 to 6.

MOLE POBLANO PARA GALLINA O GUAJOLOTE
Mole Sauce for Turkey or Chicken

Mole sauce (pronounced moh-leh) sounds rather complicated, but it
really is not difficult to make. The blend of all the spices and other
flavors gives it its individuality and goodness. The recipe makes
enough sauce for a 10 or 12 lb. turkey.

1 turkey, or 2 fricassee
chickens, cut in pieces
30 chiles mulatos
20 chiles anchos
10 chiles pasilla
1 tablespoon mixed seeds
from chiles
½ cup almonds, not
blanched
1 tortilla
2 French rolls
1 onion, peeled
1 clove garlic, peeled
2 whole black peppers
(pepper corns)

Pinch of anise seed
Pinch of cilantro
1 tablespoon sesame seed
1 quarter Mexican chocolate
(Mexican chocolate comes
in rounds marked in quar-
ters)
4 to 6 cups hot chicken or
turkey broth
½ cup lard or oil
Pinch of comino powder
(cumin)
1 teaspoon sugar
Salt to taste
Pinch of powdered cloves

Simmer the cut-up turkey or chicken in water to cover until tender,
adding salt to taste. While it is cooking, wash and dry the three kinds
of dry chiles. (They are different in flavor and color; all can be bought
at Mexican food stores, where you will buy many of the other ingredients called for.) Place the chiles in a dry, heavy skillet and toast them
lightly, then remove seeds. Soak the chiles in water to cover. Toast the

74

tablespoon of chile seeds with the almonds in a dry skillet until brown. Fry the tortilla crisp in a little oil; cut rolls in halves and fry until brown. Now grind all these ingredients, including the soaked chiles, also the onion, garlic, black pepper, anise, cilantro, sesame seed, and chocolate very fine, to the consistency of paste. Add turkey or chicken broth to make amount of sauce you wish, then strain it. Heat the lard or oil and add the sauce to the oil; also the comino, cloves, sugar and salt. Put the pieces of turkey or chicken into the sauce, heat thoroughly, and serve. Serves 10 to 12.

P. S. If this seems too much trouble, you can buy canned Mole Sauce at Mexican food stores!

GALLINA CON TOMATE Y PIMIENTOS MORRONES
Chicken with Tomato and Pimientos

1 fricassee chicken, cut in pieces
1 No. 2 can solid pack tomatoes
1 medium-sized onion, minced
4 tablespoons oil
2 cloves garlic
1 can pimientos
Salt and pepper to taste

Cook the chicken in hot water to which you have added salt, pepper, ½ cup diced celery, 1 carrot, sliced, and 1 tablespoon parsley. When chicken is tender, remove from broth. Force the tomatoes through a sieve. Fry the chopped onion in the oil, then add the tomato puree and the garlic mashed into a paste. Combine the mixture with the chicken and about ½ cup of the chicken broth. Cook, covered, for 30 minutes. Ten minutes before serving, season well and add the pimientos cut in cubes or strips. Serves 6.

POLLO EN CACEROLA A LA ESPANOLA
Chicken in Casserole, Spanish Style

1 roasting chicken (medium-sized) cut in pieces
½ cup water
¼ cup melted butter
2 tablespoons flour
½ teaspoon thyme
Salt and pepper
2 tablespoons minced parsley
1 bay leaf
½ cup white table wine

Wash chicken and place in casserole; add water, and melted butter mixed with flour and thyme, and salt and pepper to taste. Place in a fairly hot oven (400°); uncovered. When top pieces are brown, turn so that the bottom pieces may also brown. Then add parsley, bay leaf and wine, cover, and cook in a moderate oven (350°) until chicken is tender—about 1 hour. Serves 4.

POLLOS EN SALSA DE JEREZ
Chicken with Sherry Sauce

½ cup butter	¼ cup minced parsley
1 large onion, minced	1 cup Sherry wine
(green onions are nice)	2 bay leaves
3 cloves garlic, minced	2 frying chickens, prepared
	for roasting

Melt butter, add onion, garlic, and parsley and cook gently about 5 minutes. Add sherry and bay leaves and cook for 10 minutes. Strain, saving the highly flavored sherry to use later. Put the onion and garlic inside the fryers to flavor them, rub with the butter. Brown in a fairly hot oven (425°) for 15 minutes, then lower heat to 350° and bake about 45 minutes. Baste frequently with the strained Sherry. Serves 4 to 6, depending on size of chickens.

GUAJOLOTE RELLENO A LA MEXICANA
Stuffed Turkey, Mexican Style

1 turkey—about 15 lbs.	½ pound prunes, soaked and
10 apples, peeled, cored,	pitted
quartered	½ cup blanched almonds
½ pound butter or mar-	1 teaspoon sugar
garine	Salt, pepper, nutmeg to taste
½ pound "Pound Cake"	1 pint Sherry wine

Clean and prepare the turkey in the usual manner, rubbing the inside of the turkey with melted butter. To prepare this very unusual stuffing, cook apples slightly. Melt the butter or margarine, and add the crumbled pound cake, apples, prunes and almonds. Season with sugar, nutmeg, salt and pepper. Mix well and add the Sherry wine. Truss and prepare bird for roasting, rub lightly with oil, place in an open roasting pan and roast in a moderately slow oven (325°), allowing 20 minutes to the pound.

Chapter Eight
ENSALADAS - Salads

CON BUENA HAMBRE NO HAY MAL PAN. (If you are really hungry, anything tastes good.)

ENSALADAS—Salads

*I*N MEXICO *the first-course salad, as we know it in California, is very rare. When Mexicans serve salad they put it on the table in a platter or bowl along with the entree. The most popular Mexican salads are made with avocado or combinations of vegetables. And always the serving dish is well rubbed with garlic. Perhaps one reason Mexicans do not feel the need of more raw salads is because chile peppers, which they eat so freely, are rich in vitamins A and C.*

GUACAMOLE
Avocado Salad

1 fresh tomato, peeled	1 tablespoon vinegar
2 avocados	Salt and pepper to taste
½ onion, minced	Chopped green chile to taste

Mash tomato and avocados together, and blend in remaining ingredients. If desired, the seeds of pomegranate may be added to the above mixture. **Guacamole** can be enjoyed best with stuffed, warmed tortillas.

ENSALADA DE AGUACATE
Mexican Avocado Salad

3 avocados	French dressing
1 cup pineapple cubes	Lettuce
2 oranges, peeled and cut into pieces	Fresh mint

Cut avocados in half lengthwise, and scoop out pulp with a French ball cutter. Save shells. Combine avocado balls with other fruit, and marinate in French dressing about 20 minutes. Fill avocado shells and serve on lettuce. Garnish with fresh mint. Serves 6.

JAIBA Y ALCACHOFA
Artichoke and Crab Salad

1 cup diced, cooked arti- choke hearts	1 cup mayonnaise
	½ cup tomato catsup
1 cup crabmeat	Dash of Tabasco sauce
½ cup heavy cream, whipped	Salt and pepper

Mix artichokes and crabmeat; chill. Combine whipped cream, mayonnaise, catsup, Tabasco sauce, salt and pepper; chill. When ready to serve, combine sauce with the artichoke and crab mixture. Serve on lettuce. Serves 6. If desired, use cooked shrimp or lobster meat instead of crab, and add ¼ cup chopped ripe or green olives.

TOMATE RELLENO CON CAMARON
Stuffed Tomatoes with Shrimps

6 tomatoes, skinned and chilled	3 tablespoons tomato catsup
	1 tablespoon vinegar
1 cup canned shrimps	Grated onion to taste
½ cup finely minced celery	Mayonnaise

Hollow out tomatoes. Combine shrimps, celery, catsup, vinegar, and onion, adding enough mayonnaise to hold mixture together. Stuff tomatoes with the mixture, and serve on shredded lettuce with French dressing. Serves 6.

ENSALADA DE LENGUA Y COL
Tongue and Cabbage Salad

1 head cabbage	1 green pepper, chopped
1 cup diced cooked tongue	1 sweet red pepper, chopped
1 cup diced cooked ham	½ an onion, chopped

Shred cabbage as for coleslaw. Add next 5 ingredients and blend with French dressing, or with mayonnaise if preferred. Serves 8.

ENSALADA ESPANOLA DE CARNE DE RES
Spanish Beef Salad

6 slices cold roast beef	6 thick slices tomato
Tomato French dressing	6 onion slices
1 head lettuce, shredded	6 green pepper rings

Cut roast beef into long narrow strips. Marinate in dressing for 1 hour. Toss in salad bowl with lettuce and additional dressing. Border bowl with alternating slices of tomato, onion and green pepper. Serves 6.

AGUACATE MEDIA LUNA
Avocado Crescents

Cut fruit in half lengthwise and remove seed. Pare and slice each half crosswise to form crescents. Sprinkle with lemon juice and salt. Arrange on salad greens with rounded edges overlapping, and garnish with a section of lemon. For variation, insert wedges of tomato and serve with French dressing.

ENSALADA DE AGUACATES RELLENOS
Stuffed Avocados

3 avocados
1 head Romaine lettuce
½ cup finely minced celery
½ cup cubed apple
½ cup chopped, blanched almonds
¼ cup French dressing
¼ cup mayonnaise
Paprika to taste

Cut avocados in half lengthwise and peel. Place on individual plates lined with Romaine lettuce. Combine celery, apple and almonds, adding the French dressing and mixing well. Fill avocado halves with the mixture, top with a little mayonnaise, and sprinkle with paprika. Serves 6.

TOMATE Y AGUACATE EN FUENTE
Tomato Avocado Salad Bowl

1 avocado
4 tomatoes, peeled and cut into eighths
½ head lettuce
½ head chicory
½ bunch watercress
French dressing

Cut avocado in half lengthwise and remove seed; peel, then cut into crescents. Put into bowl which has been rubbed with a cut clove of garlic. Add tomato eighths and cut greens, and toss all together. Add French dressing to taste. If desired, lemon juice may be used instead of vinegar in the French dressing.

BETABEL RELLENO
Stuffed Beet Salad

Select beets as uniform in size as possible, and cook whole, skin, chill, scoop out centers. Chop celery very fine with beet centers, and combine with peas or any other leftover vegetable. Add vinegar, a little mayonnaise, and salt and pepper to taste. Fill cavities with this mixture, and serve on shredded lettuce.

ENSALADA DE PIMIENTO Y QUESO
Green Pepper and Cheese Salad

2 large green peppers	Salt and pepper to taste
1 (3-oz.) package cream cheese	1 head Romaine lettuce
	½ cup French dressing
2 tablespoons cream	½ cup mayonnaise
12 ripe olives, chopped	Paprika

Cut tops off peppers and remove seeds. Boil peppers for 3 minutes and drain well. Combine cream cheese, cream, olives, and salt and pepper to taste. Stuff peppers with this mixture, pressing it in tightly, and place in the refrigerator to chill. When ready to serve, arrange Romaine lettuce on 4 salad plates, and add French dressing. Cut peppers crosswise in thick slices, and place two on each plate on top of the lettuce. Garnish with mayonnaise and paprika. Serves 4.

ENSALADA DE FRIJOL
Bean Salad

3 cups canned kidney beans	5 hard-cooked eggs, sliced
½ cup chopped sweet pickle	¾ cup diced celery
1 cup mayonnaise	

Drain beans; add pickle, eggs and celery, and toss together lightly. Add mayonnaise and blend. Chill thoroughly. Serve on shredded lettuce and garnish with egg wedges. Serves 8.

ENSALADA DE FRIJOL
Mexican Pink Bean Salad

Marinate freshly cooked pink beans in French dressing, adding minced green onions to taste. Serve on shredded lettuce.

ENSALADA DE BERENJENAS
Eggplant Salad

2 eggplants	½ cup chopped celery
Lemon juice	¼ cup French dressing
Salt to taste	1 head Romaine lettuce
1 teaspoon minced onion	¼ cup mayonnaise
1 cup chopped nuts	1 hard-cooked egg, minced
10 stuffed olives	

Peel the eggplants and cut in cubes. Cook until tender, adding a little lemon juice and salt to the water. Drain and allow to cool. Mix eggplant with onion, nuts and celery; add French dressing. Place Romaine lettuce in bottom of a bowl, and put eggplant on top. Decorate with mayonnaise, minced hard-cooked egg and stuffed olives. Serves 6.

HUEVOS RELLENOS ENDIABLADOS
Deviled Stuffed Eggs

6 hard-cooked eggs   ½ a 3-oz. can deviled ham
1 tablespoon onion juice   3 to 4 tablespoons mayonnaise
Dash of Worcestershire sauce

Cut eggs in half lengthwise, remove yolks and force them through strainer. Add balance of ingredients and mix well. Fill egg whites with this mixture, and serve on shredded lettuce.

ENSALADA JARDINERA
Garden Salad

2 large potatoes, boiled and   ½ cup mayonnaise
    diced   2 tablespoons prepared
4 beets, cooked and sliced   mustard
2 canned pimientos,   1 tablespoon minced onion
    chopped   ½ teaspoon paprika
1 head Romaine lettuce,   Salt and pepper to taste
    shredded

Rub a large bowl with a cut clove of garlic and add vegetables. Combine mayonnaise, mustard, onion and paprika, and mix with vegetables. Season to taste with salt and pepper. Serves 4 or 5.

ENSALADA DE COLIFLOR
Cauliflower Salad

Cook cauliflower in salted water until tender. Cool and separate into flowerets. Serve on shredded lettuce with the following dressing: Boil 1 teaspoon paprika in ⅓ cup vinegar; cool; mix with 1 cup mayonnaise.

ENSALADA DE EJOTES
Mexican String Bean Salad

After stringing beans, cut lengthwise in halves and cook until tender. When beans are cold, add oil, vinegar, minced onion, salt and pepper to taste, and grated cheese. Mix well, and serve on lettuce.

ENSALADA DE AJO
Garlic Salad

Toast slices of French bread. Place in bottom of a bowl which has been rubbed with a cut clove of garlic. Mash additional garlic to a paste and rub on toast. Add lettuce or other greens. Pour over all a French dressing, made preferably with olive oil. Let stand a while before serving. If desired, slices of bread may be cubed after rubbing with garlic paste, then tossed with the greens.

ENSALADA DE ATUN
Tuna Salad Spanish

Mash tuna fish; add finely minced celery, grated onion, chopped pimiento, and French dressing to taste. Serve on slices of tomato, arranged on shredded lettuce.

AGUACATE Y BERRO
Avocado and Watercress

Rub a bowl with garlic; put in watercress and cubed avocado. Add French dressing and toss lightly.

JAIBA CON PAPAS
Crab with Potatoes

To 1 cup crabmeat add 2 cubed cooked potatoes, and minced celery, mayonnaise, and lemon juice to taste. Season well. Serve on slices of tomato, arranged on shredded lettuce.

ENSALADA DE CAMARON Y COL
Cabbage and Shrimps

Grate half a medium-sized cabbage, and chop 1 can of shrimps. (If fresh shrimps are used, do not chop.) Add grated onion, vinegar, oil, salt and pepper to taste. Serve on lettuce.

TOMATE RELLENO CON GUACAMOLE
Stuffed Tomato with Avocado

Skin tomatoes and chill. Hollow out and fill with Guacamole. (Recipe for Guacamole on page 79.) Serve in nests of shredded lettuce, with French dressing.

Chaper Nine

LEGUMBRES - Vegetables

AHORA ES CUANDO, CHILE VERDE, LE HAS DE DAR SABOR AL CALDO. (Now is the time, my dear, for you to season the broth.)

LEGUMBRES—Vegetables

URING the years that I managed my Mexican restaurant (Elena's Mexican Village) in San Francisco, I had many compliments on my vegetable dishes. Everyone seemed to like my tasty sauces and combinations. Now that I am preparing meals only for my own family, I still follow my old standby recipes. Maybe once in a while I waste some vitamins by cooking a vegetable somewhat longer than the new rules call for, but the results are good; therefore, I don't worry. Like all Mexican families, we like good food and eat lots of it, and in that way we seem to get enough of the vitamins we need.

ALCACHOFAS EMPANIZADAS
Breaded Artichokes

8 medium-sized artichokes	Grated cheese
3 eggs	Salt and pepper
Fine bread crumbs	

Wash artichokes, cook until tender in boiling salted water. Drain. When cold cut in halves lengthwise, dip in beaten eggs, then into bread crumbs which have been mixed with grated cheese. Salt and pepper to taste. Repeat this egging-and-crumbing, and fry in a generous amount of oil in a skillet until brown on both sides. Serves 8.

ALCACHOFAS RELLENAS
Baked Stuffed Artichokes

Cut the tops off large artichokes and spread the leaves apart. Then take some garlic sausage, chop up very fine with some onions and parsley, and force this between the leaves of the artichokes. Bake in a pan containing plenty of olive oil, in a moderate oven (350°) about 30 minutes, or until tender. Keep basting them with the oil.

TORTA DE ALCACHOFA
Artichokes with Egg

12 baby artichokes
¼ cup oil
1 clove garlic
1 small onion, minced

1 sprig fresh albahaca (sweet basil) if possible
Salt and pepper to taste
4 eggs
3 tablespoons grated cheese

Wash artichokes and remove tough outside leaves, then slice into rounds, discarding any tough leaves as you cut. Put oil in pan, add peeled whole clove of garlic, minced onion and sliced artichokes. Cover and let cook until artichokes are tender. Beat eggs well, add cheese, pour over artichokes and with a fork keep stirring as you would scrambled eggs. Cook until egg is well cooked. Serves 4 to 6.

ALCACHOFAS A LA VINAGRETA
Artichokes in Vinegar Sauce

12 small artichokes
2 onions cut into rings (preferably red onions)
¾ cup oil

½ cup vinegar
1 teaspoon prepared mustard
Salt and pepper

Wash artichokes and cook in boiling salted water until hearts are tender. Drain. In a deep bowl arrange alternate layers of artichokes and onion rings. Mix remaining ingredients, pour over the artichokes and onions and let stand several hours before serving. Turn artichokes occasionally so that they will be well coated with the dressing. Serves 3 or 4.

COL RELLENA
Stuffed Cabbage

1 large head of cabbage
½ pound ground veal
½ pound ground pork

¼ pound boiled ham, minced
3 teaspoons salt
¼ teaspoon pepper

Place head of cabbage in boiling salted water in a large kettle long enough for its leaves to open. Remove from kettle, drain, and let cool enough to handle. Mix ground veal, pork, ham, salt and pepper. Open the cabbage leaves enough to insert a thin layer of this mixture between each 2 leaves. Tie cabbage together with string, put back into the boiling water and cook until meat is done—about 40 minutes. When cooked, drain and place immediately on hot platter, pouring white sauce or tomato sauce over all. Serves 6.

TORTA DE ESPARRAGO
Asparagus with Egg

1 pound green asparagus	Pinch of tomillo (thyme)
¼ cup oil	Salt and pepper to taste
1 small onion, minced	3 eggs
1 clove garlic, peeled	3 tablespoons grated cheese

Wash and cut asparagus in inch pieces. Put oil in pan, add asparagus, minced onion, whole clove of garlic, thyme, salt and pepper to taste. Cover and cook slowly until asparagus is tender. Remove garlic. Beat eggs well; add cheese and pour over asparagus. Keep stirring with a fork as you would scrambled eggs until egg is well cooked. Serves 4.

COLES MORADAS CON VINO
Red Cabbage in Wine

2 red cabbages	1 cup red table wine
(about 4 pounds)	1 cup beef stock
4 tablespoons butter	Salt and pepper
or margarine	½ teaspoon sugar

Shred cabbage very fine. Place in saucepan with butter or margarine. Cook slowly for 20 minutes. Add wine and stock; cook about 25 minutes longer, or until tender. Season with salt and pepper; add sugar last. Especially recommended with loin of pork or sausages. Serves 6.

COLECITAS DE BRUSELAS CON CASTANAS
Brussels Sprouts with Chestnuts

1 onion, minced	1 cup cooked and peeled
⅓ cup butter	chestnuts
2 cups cooked Brussels sprouts	Salt and pepper to taste

Fry onion gently in butter, being careful not to let butter brown. Add chestnuts and sprouts. Season with salt and pepper, and heat thoroughly. Serves 4.

COLECITAS DE BRUSELAS A LA MEXICANA
Brussels Sprouts, Mexican Style

4 slices bacon	1 cup tomato puree
1 small onion, minced	Salt and pepper
2 cups cooked Brussels sprouts	

Cut bacon in squares and fry; add onions, then sprouts. Now add tomato puree (made by forcing solid pack canned tomatoes through sieve), season with salt and pepper, and let cook until thoroughly heated. Serves 4.

CHILES RELLENOS
Stuffed Peppers

Cut Monterey cream cheese into oblongs about 1 inch wide and 2 inches long and ½ inch thick. Around each piece of cheese wrap a strip of peeled green chile, either canned or fresh. Have ready a batter made as follows: Allow 1 egg to each 2 whole peppers (chiles), and 1 tablespoon flour to each egg. Separate eggs; beat whites until stiff, then lightly fold in beaten yolks and flour. Drop the cheese-stuffed peppers into the mixture one at a time. Pick up with a spoon and place in a frying pan with plenty of moderately hot oil, about 1½ inches deep, and fry until golden brown on both sides. Drain on absorbent paper and let stand. Shortly before serving time, make a thin sauce as follows: Mince half an onion and 1 clove garlic fine, and fry in a little oil. Strain 2 cups of solid pack tomatoes into the mixture, forcing the puree through the sieve; then add 2 cups of any kind of stock, preferably chicken. When boiling, season with 1½ teaspoons salt, ½ teaspoon pepper and 1 teaspoon oregano, which is rubbed between the palms of the hands into the sauce. When ready to serve, put the peppers into the boiling sauce just long enough to heat them through—about 5 minutes. They puff up when heated this way. Peppers may be fixed several hours or even a day ahead of time, and heated in the sauce just before serving.

CHILES VERDES RELLENOS CON SARDINA
Green Chiles Stuffed with Sardines

1 dozen long green chiles or bell peppers	1 can boneless sardine fillets
½ cup vinegar	1 teaspoon oregano
3 tablespoons oil	Salt and pepper
2 fresh peeled tomatoes	Grated cheese
1 medium-sized onion, minced	2 large onions, sliced in rings

Place peppers under broiler, turn on all sides. When well heated, place in paper bag and close so as to steam for 15 minutes, then peel off the thin skin. Remove seeds, being careful not to break the peppers. Soak peeled peppers in vinegar and oil overnight. Next day stuff the peppers with chopped tomatoes, minced onion, sardines, oregano, and some of the vinegar and oil in which you soaked the peppers. (Mix all ingredients well, adding salt and pepper to taste.) Place on platter, sprinkle with grated cheese; garnish with rings of onions which have been soaked in salt water and a little vinegar for at least an hour. These stuffed chiles may be used as a salad or relish, or served with refried beans. The long green chiles are hot; the bell peppers are not.

CHILE CON QUESO
Green Chile with Cheese

1 small onion, minced
2 tablespoons butter
½ cup tomato puree
2 green chiles, peeled (if desired more can be added)

½ pound Monterey cream cheese
1 cup table cream
Salt and pepper to taste

Brown onion in butter; add tomato puree and chopped chile. Simmer for 15 minutes. When ready to serve, add cut-up cheese and cream to the sauce, and heat until cheese melts. Serve with refried beans and tortillas. Makes 4 servings.

ARROZ CON CHILES RELLENOS
Mexican Rice with Stuffed Chiles

2 cups uncooked rice
½ cup oil
6 white onions, cut in quarters
6 green chiles (canned)

½ pound Monterey Cream cheese
4 cups beef stock, boiling hot
¼ cup butter or margarine
Salt and pepper to taste

Fry unwashed rice in oil, but do not brown. When cold, place a layer of rice in saucepan with a tight cover; add a layer of onion, then a layer of chiles which have been stuffed with cheese. Repeat this procedure until all ingredients are used, making the last layer rice. Dot with the butter, pour well-seasoned stock over all, cover tightly and cook slowly on top of stove for half an hour. Serves 8.

MORE ABOUT CHILES RELLENOS

Chiles Rellenos is a typical Mexican recipe, yet it can be used by the average family in any part of the country by following the suggestions listed below. If green peeled chiles are not available, or you do not desire to have a hot dish, use canned pimientos or fresh bell peppers, skinned, following the recipe for Chiles Rellenos given in this book. The batter used in this recipe may also be used for coating of zucchini. If Monterey cheese is not available, American cheese may be used. The same batter may be used to make shrimp fritters. A Mexican corn fritter may be made in the following manner: Fry 2 tablespoons minced onion and 2 tablespoons chopped bell pepper in 2 tablespoons butter, until tender; add 1 cup canned whole kernel corn and season to taste. When cold, drop by spoonfuls into the above batter, then fry like fritters. These are delicious as a vegetable, served hot.

BERENJENAS RELLENAS
Stuffed Eggplant

3 medium-sized eggplants	2 eggs
¼ pound boiled ham, minced	½ cup grated cheese
½ cup bread crumbs	¼ cup butter
1 teaspoon minced parsley	Salt and pepper to taste
2 tablespoons minced onion	

Cook eggplants, whole, in boiling salted water for 15 minutes. Cut each in two lengthwise; remove pulp; drain. Combine remaining ingredients with the pulp. Mix well and use to refill the eggplant shells. Place in shallow buttered baking dish and have ready the following sauce:

1 tablespoon minced onion	½ cup tomato puree
1 clove garlic, minced	½ cup beef stock
2 tablespoons oil	Salt and pepper to taste
	1 bay leaf

Fry minced onion and garlic in oil until soft; add remaining ingredients and simmer 15 minutes. Pour over stuffed eggplants and bake in a moderately hot oven (375°) until lightly browned on top — about 20 minutes. Serves 6.

PIMIENTOS MORRONES RELLENOS
Stuffed Pimientos

1 cup corn niblets	2 eggs, beaten
1 tablespoon melted butter	6 canned pimientos
Salt and pepper	1 cup cream

Mix corn, butter, eggs, and salt and pepper to taste, and use to stuff pimientos. Arrange in buttered baking dish, and bake in a moderate oven (350°) until stuffing is firm. Remove from oven and pour over all the cream which has been seasoned with salt and pepper. Return to oven for a few minutes longer to allow cream to heat. Serve hot. Serves 6.

PIMIENTOS RELLENOS CON ARROZ
Stuffed Peppers with Rice

6 uniform-sized bell peppers, green or red	1 cup uncooked rice
	¼ cup oil
1 pound raw ham (ground)	Salt and pepper

Remove seeds from peppers at the top, being careful not to make too big an opening. Fry the minced ham wtih the dry rice in the hot oil; stuff peppers half full with this mixture (the rice expands). Butter very well a deep casserole, place the peppers in it, cover with hot water, season with salt and pepper, and bake in a moderate oven (350°) approximately 45 minutes. Serves 6.

CHILES VERDES EN CACEROLA
Bell Pepper Casserole

6 bell peppers	1½ cups cubed American
6 eggs	cheese
2 cups milk	Salt and pepper to taste

Place bell peppers in the broiling oven and turn on all sides until skins begin to blister; place in a paper bag, close and let stand for 15 minutes, then peel off thin skin. Remove seeds and cut peppers into strips. Butter a casserole well. Put in it first a layer of peppers, then a layer of American cheese, repeating this until all the peppers and cheese are used. Beat eggs well, add milk, season with salt and pepper and pour over peppers and cheese. Bake in a slow oven (300°) for 1 hour, or until firm in the center. This will serve 8.

TORTA DE CHICHAROS
Peas with Eggs

¼ cup oil or butter	2 eggs
½ an onion, minced	1 tablespoon grated
1 cup shelled fresh peas	cheese (optional)
1 slice bread, soaked in water	Salt and pepper

Heat oil in saucepan, add minced onion and peas, and cook, covered, until tender. Add bread which has been drained dry. Beat eggs, add cheese, then add to peas, and stir with fork until eggs are cooked. Serves 2 or 3.

COLIFLOR EMPANIZADA
Breaded Cauliflower

Separate a cold cooked cauliflower into flowerets. Dip each into well beaten egg; roll in bread crumbs mixed with grated cheese; fry in oil until delicately browned. Serves 4.

COLIFLOR FRIA CON AGUACATE
Cold Cauliflower with Avocado

1 large cauliflower	⅓ cup blanched almonds
6 tablespoons oil	3 avocados, peeled and mashed
3 tablespoons vinegar	1 small onion, minced
Salt and pepper	Dash of nutmeg

Cook cauliflower and place in deep dish. Mix and pour over it the oil and vinegar, salt and pepper. When cold, place on a round platter. Make a paste of the almonds mixed with mashed avocados to which minced onion, salt and nutmeg have been added. Cover the cauliflower completely with this paste, and garnish with radish rosettes and rounds of tomato. Serves 6.

PIMIENTOS FRESCOS ASADOS
Broiled Fresh Pimientos
Place fresh pimientos under the broiler, turning on all sides until skin blisters. Place in paper bag, close and let steam for 15 minutes, then peel off thin skin; remove seeds and cut pimientos in strips. Rub a bowl with garlic, put in the pimientos, then add oil, vinegar, salt and pepper to taste, and let stand 2 hours before using. These are delightful.

CACEROLA CON PAPAS Y QUESO
Potatoes with Cheese in Casserole

6 large potatoes	2 eggs, beaten
1/4 cup butter	1 onion, minced
Salt and pepper	1 cup cubed American cheese

Boil and mash potatoes; add butter, salt and pepper and eggs, beating well. Stir in onions, then add cheese. Heap in a buttered casserole, dot top with butter and bake in a moderately hot oven (375°) for 30 minutes. Serves 6.

PAPAS RELLENAS CON HUEVOS
Potatoes Stuffed with Egg

6 large potatoes	Salt and pepper to taste
6 eggs	1/2 cup grated cheese
1/4 cup butter	

Cook potatoes in their jackets, then peel. Hollow out a cavity in the long side of each potato, being careful not to cut through to the bottom. Place potatoes in baking pan, propping them up with pieces which were cut out. Drop an egg into each cavity, dot with butter, add salt and pepper to taste, and sprinkle with the grated cheese. Bake in a moderately hot oven (375°) for 15 minutes. If desired mounds of mashed potatoes may be used instead. Serves 6.

GORDITAS DE PAPA
Potato Patties

3 large potatoes	1/3 cup oil
1/2 pound masa (Mexican corn meal purchased at Mexican store)	Guacamole (see recipe in chapter on salads)
3 tablespoons grated cheese	1 cup diced cooked chicken

Steam potatoes and peel. Mash well and mix thoroughly with masa and cheese. Form into small patties with deep indentation in center. When ready to serve, fry in hot oil. Fill centers with guacamole and chicken which may be seasoned to your individual taste. Serves 6.

MANZANITAS DE PAPA
Imitation Apples

Cook and peel uniform-sized new potatoes; brown in deep oil. Remove carefully; turn each potato into an "apple" by tucking a clove into the top for a stem, and dusting with paprika to provide color. Makes a beautiful garnish for a roast.

COLACHE
Summer Squash, Mexican Style

4 large summer squash	¼ cup butter or margarine
4 ears corn	1 small onion, chopped fine
3 fresh tomatoes, peeled	Salt and pepper

Wash summer squash and cut into small pieces. Cut kernels from the ears of corn; cut tomatoes into cubes. Place butter in saucepan and in it fry onion till brown. Add summer squash, corn and tomatoes; season to taste, cover, and cook slowly 35 to 40 minutes. Shake pan occasionally to avoid scorching. Serves 6.

TORTA DE CALABAZAS
Casserole, Mexican Style

2 pounds zucchini	½ cup grated cheese
1 onion, minced	Salt and pepper
1 clove garlic, minced	2 eggs, separated
2 tablespoons oil	2 tablespoons butter
3 tomatoes, peeled	2 tablespoons bread crumbs
1 tablespoon minced parsley	

Cook zucchini tender, drain and chop. Fry onion and garlic in oil; add chopped tomato and parsley, then add zucchini and grated cheese. Season to taste. Beat egg whites stiff but not dry. Beat egg yolks, then add to whites and beat well. Butter a casserole and sprinkle in half of the bread crumbs. Put in a layer of egg batter, then one of zucchini mixture, and repeat this procedure until all ingredients are used. Over top layer sprinkle remaining bread crumbs, dot with butter, and bake in a moderately hot oven (375°) until brown. Serves 6.

CALABAZAS CON ELOTE
Italian Squash with Corn

1 pound zucchini	¼ cup oil
1 medium onion	Pinch of sugar
2 fresh tomatoes, peeled	Salt and pepper
3 ears corn	

Wash and cut zucchini in rings. Mince onion, chop tomatoes, cut corn from cobs, add oil and seasonings; mix well and cook, covered, 20 to 30 minutes. Serves 6.

TORTAS DE CALABAZA CON QUESO
Zucchini Fritters with Cheese

5 eggs, separated	½ an onion, minced
5 tablespoons flour	1 cup tomato puree
3 large zucchinis	2 cups water or stock
1 pound Monterey cream	(chicken)
cheese	1 teaspoon oregano
1 cup oil	Salt and pepper

Fritters: Beat egg whites very stiff, but not dry; beat egg yolks separately and fold into whites, then fold in flour. Parboil zucchini and cut into rounds; place a piece of Monterey cream cheese (size desired) between 2 rounds of zucchini, drop into batter one at a time. Fry in hot oil, being careful that it is not too hot, so as to keep the egg from becoming hard. When gold colored, remove from oil, drain on absorbent paper. **Sauce:** If too much oil is left after frying fritters, pour off all but ¼ cup in which brown the onion, then add tomato puree and stock or water; rub oregano between palms of hands into sauce, season with salt and pepper and cook for 20 minutes. Just before serving, drop fritters into sauce, let them heat through thoroughly and serve. Serves 6 to 8.

EJOTES CON CHILE COLORADO
String Beans with Red Chile Sauce

2 tablespoons oil	1 pound string beans, split
8-oz. bottle of red chile	lengthwise and cooked
sauce (purchased at	2 eggs
Mexican store)	Salt and pepper

Heat oil and chile sauce in big frying pan and cook a few minutes, then add string beans and heat thoroughly. Just before serving, break eggs into pan, season to taste, and stir them with a fork as you would scrambled eggs. Serves 6.

CALABAZA ENMIELADA
Banana Squash with Brown Sugar

1 small banana squash	1 pound brown sugar
(5 to 6 pounds)	¼ cup water

Wipe the squash with a damp cloth. Cut into quarters, or smaller pieces, as desired. Remove seeds and pack brown sugar on top of each piece of squash. Place in a pan that can be tightly covered, and pour the water into the pan. Cover and cook on top of stove until tender After this is done, if the syrup is not thick enough, add more sugar to suit your taste. The typical Mexican way of serving this squash is to scoop the cooked squash into a deep bowl, pour the syrup over the top and add some milk. It is a delightful breakfast dish.

Chapter Ten

FRIJOLES - Beans

GRANO A GRANO LLENA EL BUCHE LA GALLINA. (Grain by grain
the chicken fills its gullet.)

FRIJOLES—Beans

A MEAL *is not a meal in Mexico unless beans are served in some form or other. Generally they are served just before the dessert, and the favorite way is refried. Many characteristic dishes are accompanied by beans; for instance, tacos, tostadas, and enchiladas. Some people believe that cooking beans takes no skill at all, but in Mexico everyone knows it to be an art! There the beans are not soaked unless they are very old. They are put on to cook in warm water, which prevents the skins from getting tough. They are simmered, never boiled, all through the cooking, with frequent stirring; and they are cooked until they begin to break open. Salt is added during the last half hour of cooking. It should be remembered that Mexicans use a small red bean. Here in the United States the Mexican pink bean is always used in typical Mexican dishes.*

BASIC MEXICAN BEAN RECIPE

Put 2 cups Mexican pink beans on to cook in 5 cups lukewarm water, and cook gently, covered, until tender (1½ to 2 hours). Add salt to taste during the last half hour of cooking. Be sure to stir beans occasionally so they will cook evenly. In frying pan heat ½ cup bacon drippings (or lard or oil). (Bacon drippings improve the flavor.) Drain some of the beans (saving liquid), add to hot fat and mash thoroughly. This serves to thicken the gravy. Add more liquid, a little at a time, repeating the procedure until all beans and all liquid have been used. Then continue cooking, stirring frequently, until mixture is of thickness desired. The stirring is important since the beans burn easily. Serves 4 to 6.

A nice variation for the use of beans is made by frying onions, garlic, bell peppers, and chile powder dissolved in a small amount of hot beef stock; then add kidney beans and hominy in equal proportions and heat thoroughly.

FRIJOLES REFRITOS
Refried Beans

Heat additional oil in frying pan; add mashed and fried beans (see basic bean recipe), and cook, stirring, until beans are completely dry. The result is refried beans.

FRIJOLES REFRITOS CON QUESO
Refried Beans with Cheese

Follow same procedure for refried beans, adding cubed Monterey cream cheese to beans, allowing time for the cheese to melt. They are then ready to serve.

FRIJOLES CHINITOS
Crisp Mexican Refried Beans

Re-fry refried beans until crisp!

FRIJOLES PUERCOS
Beans with Sardines, Mexican Style

Use refried beans, adding pieces of sardines and strips of green chiles (fresh or canned) to suit your individual taste, or cubed Monterey cheese; fry until hot.

NOTE: *If you live where pink beans are not available, or you do not wish to cook beans, a substitute for refried beans may be obtained by using canned kidney beans in the following manner: Heat 4 tablespoons fat and in it mash 1 can drained kidney beans, using potato masher; gradually adding the liquid drained from the beans. Cook until all fat has been absorbed. In my opinion the real refried beans are superior, but these are very good.*

FRIJOLES CON BOLITAS DE MASA
Beans with Mexican Cornmeal Dumplings

Follow basic recipe for Mexican beans, adding an extra cup of water. When beans are done, make dumplings: Mix thoroughly 1 pound masa (fresh-ground corn meal—bought at Mexican stores), 3 tablespoons melted butter, salt to taste. Make into small balls, size of a large cherry. Press center of balls with thumb, to make a thimble-like shape; drop into hot beans and cook, covered, for 20 minutes. (Reason for pressing balls is so that they will cook through.)

Chile beans may be varied by making meat balls out of ground meat and cooking them right in with the beans. The canned kidney beans may also be used, seasoned with chile powder.

MOLE DE FRIJOL
Beans in Mole Sauce

1 pound pink Mexican beans
½ cup grated cheese
1 medium-sized onion, minced
2 tablespoons melted butter
2 eggs, beaten light

¼ cup bread crumbs
4 chorizos (Mexican sausages)
½ cup prepared red chile sauce (bought at Mexican stores)
Salt and pepper to taste

Cook beans, following basic Mexican recipe (see page 99). Make sure that beans are thoroughly mashed and quite dry. To this add grated cheese, eggs, minced onion and butter, and mix well. Season with salt and pepper. Sprinkle a well-greased loaf pan with bread crumbs, add above mixture, reserving some of the crumbs for topping. Bake 45 minutes to 1 hour in moderate oven (350°). Skin the chorizos, break up and fry in a little oil. Turn loaf out on hot platter, sprinkle fried chorizos around it on the platter. Heat chile sauce and pour it over the chorizos. Serves 6.

FRIJOLES PUERCOS ESTILO SINALOA
Beans, Sinaloa Style

½ pound bacon
4 cups cooked Mexican beans (save some of the liquid)

½ pound Monterey cheese (not too dry)
3 balls chorizo
1 can sardines in tomato sauce

Cut bacon in small pieces; fry until crisp. To this add beans, a few at a time, mashing after each addition and adding some of the bean liquid. Cook to a thick gravy, then add cheese which has been cubed and the chorizos which have been removed from casings and fried. Lastly add the sardines cut in pieces. Heat and serve on hot platter decorated with strips of tosdadas which may be used as "spoons" when eating the beans. Serves 8.

HABAS CON JAMON Y VINO BLANCO
Horse Beans with Ham and White Wine

1 onion, minced
1 clove garlic, minced
4 tablespoons oil
¾ cup cubed smoked ham
2 tablespoons minced parsley

2 cups fresh horse beans (shelled and washed)
1 cup white table wine
Salt and pepper

Fry onion and garlic in the oil; add ham and parsley and cook for a few minutes; add horse beans, wine, salt and pepper. Cover very tightly and simmer slowly until beans are tender—about 40 minutes. Serves 4.

FRIJOLES DE LA OLLA
Boiled Beans, Mexican Style

Put 2 cups Mexican pink beans to cook in 6 cups lukewarm water; simmer, covered, until tender. Salt the last half hour of cooking. Be sure to stir beans occasionally, so they will cook evenly. Serve in soup plates, with rings of green onions, grated cheese, and oregano to taste. Liquid chile sauce may be added if desired.

FRIJOLES BLANCOS CON CHORIZO
White Beans with Chorizo, Spanish Style

1 onion, minced
1 clove garlic, finely minced
¼ cup oil (preferably olive oil)
¼ cup chopped parsley
3 tablespoons tomato sauce

6 cups warm water
2 cups white beans, washed and soaked overnight (drain)
3 chorizos Espanoles (Spanish sausages)
Salt and pepper to taste

Fry onion and garlic in oil until soft. Add parsley, tomato sauce, water, and soaked beans, and whole chorizos; cook, covered, until beans are tender—about 2 hours. Taste before adding salt and pepper, because chorizos sometimes supply sufficient seasoning. Serves 6.

GARBANZOS A LA ESPANOLA CON TOMATE
Chick Peas with Tomatoes, Spanish Style

1 cup of garbanzos (chick peas)
3 cups water
1 clove garlic
1 small onion, minced

1½ cups tomato puree
¼ cup oil
Salt and pepper to taste
1 can pimientos (if desired)

Soak garbanzos in lukewarm salted water over night. Drain and add 3 cups of water, minced garlic and onion. Add oil, and salt and pepper to taste. When beans are almost done, drain liquid and add tomato (solid-pack canned tomatoes, forced through a sieve); continue cooking until tender. If pimientos are being used, cut them in strips and add 10 minutes before serving. Serves 4.

SOPA DE TORTILLA (Tortilla Soup)
COLIFLOR FRIA CON AGUACATE
(Salad of Cold Cauliflower with Avocado)
POLLOS BORRACHOS (Chicken Roasters, Drunkard Style)
COLACHE (Summer Squash, Mexican)
BUDIN DE RON (Rum Pudding)   Coffee

Chapter Eleven
POSTRES - Desserts

VALE MAS QUE SOBRE PAN Y NO QUE FALTE VINO. (It is better to have bread left over than to run short of wine.)

POSTRES—Desserts

*M*EXICANS *are fond of sweets just as are their brothers across
the border. Milk desserts are very popular, and a tantalizing burnt
sugar custard with a flaming brandy sauce, known as Flan, which
originated in Spain, is an epicurean delight which will win praise
in any language. . . . Assortments of cookies are customary, but
cakes as we know them in the United States are not so popular . . .
Empanadas, little Mexican turnovers filled with jellies and jams
and dusted with sugar, are perfectly delicious and not difficult to
make. Most Mexican desserts take a great deal of preparation. But
the Mexican housewife considers the preparation of good meals
one of the most important duties of her home. However long the
preparation, the time is given gladly and the work is done with love
to please the master of the house. And so the Mexican meal ends,
as it begins, with good food, much gaiety and laughter, and a true
appreciation of love and peace in the twilight of the day.*

DULCE DE LECHE CON MANZANA O PINA
Cornstarch Pudding with Apple or Pineapple

3 eggs, well beaten
¼ cup cold milk
½ cup sugar
4 tablespoons cornstarch
⅛ teaspoon salt

1¾ cups milk, scalded
1 teaspoon vanilla
1 cup sweetened applesauce, or
1 cup diced pineapple

Mix first five ingredients together, blending well, and add to hot milk
in the top of a double boiler. Cook, stirring constantly, until pudding
thickens. Cover and cook 20 minutes longer to cook cornstarch thoroughly. Cool, and add vanilla. Place applesauce or pineapple in serving
dish and pour pudding on top. Sprinkle with powdered cinnamon and
chill before serving. Serves 4 or 5.

LECHE QUEMADA
Typical Mexican Milk Pudding

1 quart milk	¾ cup blanched almonds, ground
1 cup sugar	2 inches stick cinnamon

Place ½ quart milk in a deep saucepan with sugar, ground almonds and stick cinnamon. Cook slowly, stirring occasionally until it thickens and becomes gold colored. Then add remaining milk and continue cooking until thick, stirring from time to time. This will require about 2 hours. Chill and serve very cold. Serves 5 or 6.

For a "reasonable facsimile" of Leche Quemada, one of the most popular desserts in Mexico, drop an unopened can of sweetened condensed milk into hot water and simmer 2½ to 3 hours. Cool, remove from can and serve. A delicious combination may be made by placing on a plate a slice of pineapple, then a heaping tablespoon of this Leche Quemada, a teaspoon of whipped cream, and a sprinkling of chopped walnuts. All this may be topped with a Maraschino cherry.

LECHE DE PINA
Mexican Pineapple Milk Pudding

1 cup sugar	½ cup blanched almonds,
6 egg yolks, well beaten	ground very fine
1 quart cold milk	1 cup crushed pineapple, drained

Add sugar and beaten yolks to milk. Strain, and heat slowly, stirring constantly, until milk starts to boil. Add ground almonds and continue cooking and stirring until it thickens. Add drained pineapple and cook a few minutes longer. Pour into serving dish and sprinkle with a little powdered cinnamon. Serve very cold. Serves 6.

COCADA
Cocoanut Pudding

1 cup sugar	1 quart milk
1 cup water	3 egg yolks, well beaten
2 large sticks cinnamon	¼ cup cold milk
¼ pound grated cocoanut	

Boil sugar, water and stick cinnamon together for 10 minutes. Remove cinnamon, add cocoanut and cook until the cocoanut absorbs all of the syrup and is dry. Bring the quart of milk to a boil in a deep saucepan, add cocoanut and cook mixture for an hour, stirring occasionally to prevent sticking. Mix beaten eggs with cold milk, add to pudding and continue cooking slowly, stirring constantly, until thick, about 15 minutes. Pour onto a buttered platter and chill before serving. This pudding will keep for a long time in a cool place. Serves 6.

A nice variation for Cocada is to use 1 cup of chopped walnuts instead of coconut.

ANTE
Mexican Cornstarch Pudding

4 eggs, separated
¼ cup cold milk
1 cup sugar
¼ teaspoon salt
6 tablespoons cornstarch

1 quart milk, scalded
2 teaspoons vanilla
½ pound of pound cake
½ cup walnuts, chopped
½ cup blanched almonds, chopped

Beat egg yolks thoroughly and to them add the cold milk, sugar, salt, and cornstarch, blending well. Add egg mixture to scalded milk in the top of a double boiler and cook, stirring constantly, until thickened. Cover and cook 20 minutes longer in order to cook the cornstarch thoroughly. Line serving platter with thin slices of pound cake and sprinkle with nuts. Add vanilla to hot custard and pour over cake on platter. Beat egg whites until stiff but not dry and drop by spoonfuls on top of hot custard. Chill and serve very cold. Serves 6.

Note: A delicious variation of this pudding may be made by sprinkling ¼ cup Sherry wine or brandy over the cake.

LECHE DE CAMOTE BLANCO
Mexican Sweet Potato Milk Pudding

1 quart cold milk
3 egg yolks, well beaten
1 cup sugar
2 tablespoons cornstarch, dissolved in ¼ cup milk

1 cup cooked sweet potatoes, which have been sieved
½ cup blanched almonds, ground very fine

To the milk, add egg yolks, sugar and cornstarch. Strain, and add sweet potatoes. Place over heat and cook, stirring constantly, until thickened. Add ground almonds and cook a few minutes longer. Pour into serving dish and sprinkle with powdered cinnamon. Serve very cold. Serves 6.

CAJETA DE CAMOTE CON PIÑA
Sweet Potato and Pineapple Pudding

2 cups mashed cooked sweet potatoes
1 cup crushed pineapple, drained

1 cup sugar
¾ cup blanched almonds, ground very fine

Mix all ingredients together and cook over low heat, stirring constantly with a wooden spoon, until the bottom of the pan may be clearly seen. Place in serving dish and chill before serving. Serves 5 or 6.

Note: This pudding will keep for some time in a cold place and may also be used to stuff Empanadas—see recipe on page 119.

NATILLA
Custard with Caramel Sauce

1 quart milk	5 tablespoons cornstarch
6 egg yolks	¼ teaspoon salt
1 cup sugar	1 teaspoon vanilla

Scald 3 cups milk in the top of a double boiler. Beat egg yolks thoroughly then add remaining milk, sugar, cornstarch, and salt, mixing well. Add egg mixture to scalded milk and cook, stirring constantly, until thick. Let stand a few minutes, then add vanilla and pour onto a large platter. When cold sprinkle additional sugar over all the top. Heat an old-fashioned flat iron and press lightly over the pudding until all the sugar is caramelized. Serves 6.

ARROZ DE LECHE
Mexican Rice Pudding

6 cups boiling water	2 pieces stick cinnamon*
1 teaspoon salt	1 cup sugar
¾ cup rice	¼ teaspoon salt
1 quart milk, scalded	4 egg yolks, well beaten
	¼ cup cold milk

To briskly boiling water add the teaspoon of salt and rice, and cook for 15 minutes. Drain, and add rice to hot milk. Add stick cinnamon and cook until rice is tender, about ½ hour. Stir in sugar. Remove pudding from heat, take out stick cinnamon and add beaten egg yolks mixed with the cold milk. Return to heat and cook until thick, approximately 5 minutes longer. Pour pudding into buttered serving dish and sprinkle top with powdered cinnamon. Serves 6.

*If preferred, 1 teaspoon vanilla may be substituted for cinnamon.

TORTILLA DE RON
Rum Omelet

6 eggs, separated	2 tablespoons oil
3 tablespoons sugar	¼ cup powdered sugar
	½ cup rum

Beat whites stiff but not dry. Beat yolks until thick and lemon colored and fold into whites; add sugar slowly. Heat oil in frying pan and add egg mixture. Cook as an omelet, being careful that the frying pan is not too hot so that the omelet, when done, will be tender. Turn omelet onto a heated serving platter, sprinkle with the powdered sugar and pour the rum over all. This should be sent to the table burning. As it burns, spoon up the rum and pour over the omelet so that the alcohol will burn out and the flavoring will remain. Serves 6.

BUDIN DE RON
Rum Pudding

6 eggs, separated	1 quart milk, scalded
1 cup sugar	24 macaroons, or 1 medium
4 tablespoons cornstarch	size package
¼ cup cold milk	½ cup rum

Beat egg yolks with sugar, cornstarch, and cold milk until well blended. Then add to scalded milk in top of double boiler and cook, stirring constantly, until mixture thickens. Cover and cook 20 minutes longer to cook cornstarch thoroughly. Break macaroons into serving bowl and cover with stiffly beaten egg whites. Pour hot custard on top and when cold, fold in rum. Allow pudding to stand in refrigerator 2 or 3 hours. Sprinkle top of pudding with powdered cinnamon before serving. Serves 6.

FLAN
Caramel Custard

1¾ cups sugar	2 tall cans exaporated milk
3 egg whites	2 teaspoons vanilla
8 egg yolks	6 tablespoons brandy or rum

Put 1 cup sugar into a deep baking pan (or square loaf pan) in which custard is to be baked, and place over heat. Stir constantly until sugar melts and turns golden. Remove from heat and tip pan back and forth until it is entirely coated with caramel. Let cool while mixing custard. Beat eggs and egg yolks together well and add milk, remaining sugar and vanilla. Beat until sugar dissolves, then strain custard into caramel coated pan. Cover custard, place pan in a larger pan containing one inch of hot water, and bake in a moderate oven (350°) for 1 hour. While still hot, turn out on serving platter. When ready to serve, pour brandy or rum over pudding and send to the table burning. Serves 8.

DULCE DE SOLETAS
Lady Finger Dessert

12 lady fingers	½ cup Sherry wine
3 eggs, separated	2 tablespoons top milk
6 tablespoons sugar	

Break lady fingers into a bowl. Beat egg yolks until thick and fluffy and gradually beat in 3 tablespoons of sugar, the Sherry and top milk. Then combine with the lady fingers and place in sherbet glasses. Top each serving with meringue made by adding the remaining 3 tablespoons sugar to the stiffly beaten egg whites. Maraschino cherries may be used as a garnish. Serves 4.

LECHE EMPEDRADA
Floating Island with Raisins and Nuts

1 quart milk
4 eggs, separated
1 cup sugar
4 tablespoons cornstarch
¼ teaspoon salt

1 teaspoon vanilla
½ cup raisins, washed and
    drained
½ cup almonds or walnut pieces
6 maraschino cherries

Scald 3½ cups milk in a double boiler. Beat egg yolks thoroughly, then add remaining milk mixed with sugar, cornstarch, and salt, and mix well. Add egg mixture to scalded milk and cook, stirring constantly, until thick. Let stand a few minutes, then add vanilla and pour onto a large platter. Beat egg whites stiff and drop spoonfuls on pudding, dipping some of the hot pudding over the egg white mounds to cook meringue slightly so it won't fall. Decorate pudding with raisins and nuts and place a maraschino cherry on top of each mound of egg white. Serves 6.

BUDIN DE PAN Y NARANJA
Orange Bread Pudding

2 cups hot milk
2 cups cubed bread,
    without crust
3 tablespoons butter

½ cup sugar
2 eggs, well beaten
2 oranges, grated rind
    and juice

To the hot milk add the cubed bread, butter and sugar and let stand until cold. Then add beaten eggs, orange juice and grated rind and pour into a buttered casserole or baking pan. Bake in a moderate oven (350°) for 1 hour. Serve hot with the following sauce:

1 cup chopped raisins
1½ cups boiling water
½ cup sugar

2 tablespoons cornstarch
¼ teaspoon powdered cinnamon
1 teaspoon lemon juice

Place raisins in hot water. Then add sugar mixed with cornstarch and cinnamon, and cook, stirring, until thick. Remove from heat, add lemon juice and pour over hot pudding. Serves 6.

BUDIN DE PAN CON SALSA DE CARAMELO
Bread Pudding with Caramel Sauce

1½ cups sugar
3 cups milk
4 slices stale bread

6 eggs, well beaten
¾ cup crushed pineapple, drained
½ cup raisins

Put 1 cup of the sugar into the pan in which pudding is to be baked and place over heat. Stir until sugar dissolves into caramel. Remove from heat and tilt pan to be sure it is entirely coated with caramel. Bring milk to a boil, add bread and let stand until cool. Then mash bread and stir in eggs and remaining sugar. Add pineapple and raisins and pour into caramel coated baking pan. Place in a larger pan containing 1 inch water and bake in a slow oven (325°) for 1 hour, or until firm in the center. Turn out of pan while hot onto serving platter before caramel cools. Serve cold. Serves 8.

CAPIROTADA
Mexican Bread Pudding

1 quart water	3 bananas or apples, sliced
1 pound brown sugar	1 cup raisins
3 inches stick cinnamon	1 cup peanuts, chopped
1 whole clove	½ cup blanched almonds,
6 slices toast, cubed (or	chopped
equivalent of leftover	½ pound Monterey cheese,
pound cake)	cubed

Boil water, sugar, stick cinnamon and clove together until syrupy. Butter a casserole generously and put in a layer of bread or cake cubes. Cover with a layer of banana or apple slices and sprinkle with some of the raisins, peanuts, almonds and cheese cubes. Repeat the layers until all ingredients are used. Remove stick cinnamon and clove from syrup and pour syrup over pudding. Bake in a moderate oven (350°) about 30 minutes. Serve hot. Serves 8. In Mexico, this pudding is generally eaten during Lent.

BUDIN DE PLATANO A LA MEXICANA
Mexican Banana Pudding

Pound cake, thinly sliced	½ cup sugar
6 bananas	2 cups milk
4 eggs, separated	2 tablespoons brandy or rum

Entirely cover bottom and sides of a well buttered pudding dish or baking pan with thin slices of pound cake. Cut bananas into small pieces and sprinkle over pound cake. Beat egg yolks thoroughly with ¼ cup sugar and add to milk in the top of a double boiler. Cook, stirring constantly, until custard thickens. Add brandy or rum and pour over bananas in casserole. Beat egg whites stiff but not dry and gradually beat in remaining sugar. Cover pudding with this meringue and bake in a moderate oven (350°) until meringue is set and brown, about 20 minutes. Serves 6.

CREMA DE NARANJA
Orange Cream

6 egg yolks
3 egg whites

1 cup sugar
2 cups strained orange juice

In the top of a double boiler beat egg yolks and whites until fluffy and light. Continue beating, adding sugar gradually. Fold in orange juice and cook over boiling water until thick. Pour into serving dish and place in refrigerator until serving time. Serve very cold. Serves 6.

CHONGOS
Little Knots

1 quart milk
3 Junket tablets

2 cups water
3 cups sugar
3 inches stick cinnamon

Make Junket pudding of the milk, following recipe on the package, but using 3 Junket tablets instead of the usual amount. Pour Junket into a shallow pan and let stand until cold and solid. Then make a syrup of the water, sugar and cinnamon, boiling for 5 minutes. Remove cinnamon; add Junket by spoonfuls to boiling syrup and allow to cook gently until firm, about ½ hour. Remove cooked Chongos to a platter and continue cooking syrup if necessary, until it is thick. Pour syrup over Chongos and sprinkle powdered cinnamon over them. Serve cold. Serves 6.

SOLETAS FINGIDAS
Imitation Lady Fingers

4 eggs, separated
1 quart milk
1 stick of vanilla (available at Mexican shops)

1 cup sugar
3 tablespoons cornstarch
¼ cup cold milk

Beat egg whites until very stiff. Beat egg yolks until thick and light colored. Then fold the beaten yolks into the stiffly beaten whites. Bring the quart of milk to the boiling point and drop in vanilla stick. Drop teaspoonfuls of the egg mixture into the gently boiling milk, a few at a time, keeping them in the milk until they are cooked—about 2 to 3 minutes. As they are cooked, remove from milk and arrange on a serving platter. To the remaining hot milk add the sugar and then the cornstarch and cold milk which have been mixed together. Continue cooking, stirring constantly, until milk is thick like cornstarch pudding. Pour this sauce over the top of the cooked egg mixture, thus making the soletas. Serve cold. Serves 8.

CROQUETAS DE CREMA
Sweet Creamed Croquettes

½ cup cornstarch, mixed with
½ cup cold milk
1 cup sugar
½ teaspoon salt
4 egg yolks, well beaten

3½ cups milk, scalded
2 teaspoons vanilla
2 eggs, well beaten
2 cups sifted fine dry
    bread crumbs

Add cornstarch mixture, sugar and salt to beaten egg yolks and then add this mixture to hot milk in a double boiler. Cook, stirring constantly, until very thick. Let stand for a few minutes after removing from the heat, then add vanilla and pour this custard into a shallow pan to cool. When cold form custard into oval shaped croquettes. Dip croquettes first into beaten eggs, then roll in bread crumbs. Repeat dipping and rolling procedure to give croquettes a double coating. Just before serving fry in deep hot fat until golden brown. Serve plain or with the following sauce.

1 cup orange juice
1 cup crushed pineapple,
    undrained

½ cup sugar
½ cup raisins
¼ teaspoon salt

Blend all ingredients and cook 5 minutes. Sauce may be served either hot or cold over hot croquettes. Serves 6.

In making apple fritters, I would suggest that a delicious variation may be made by soaking the apples in brandy or whiskey for several hours. After frying, sprinkle powdered sugar and cinnamon over the hot fritters.

CAJETA DE MEMBRILLO
Pressed Quince

Wash and core quinces, being sure to remove all seeds. Steam over hot water until tender. Grind the meat of the quince very fine, including skin. Measure quince pulp and add an equal measure of sugar, mixing well. Place in a pot with a handle which is easy to hold. Cook this mixture, stirring constantly with a wooden spoon, until you can see the bottom of the pan clearly. It must be stirred constantly so that it will not burn. Empty cooked quince into a square or oblong loaf pan. When cold, turn out on a board covered with wax paper, cover quince with a cheese cloth and place in the sun. Keep in the sunshine for 2 days, turning occasionally so that all sides are exposed to the sun. This sun treatment prevents molding. Store covered in a cool, dry place. It will keep indefinitely. The best way to serve the pressed quince is with sliced American or Monterey cheese.

113

MERENGUES
Meringues

6 egg whites   1 teaspoon vanilla, or
2 cups sugar   lemon extract

Beat egg whites very stiff. Beat in sugar gradually, continuing beating until it stands in peaks. Drop meringue by spoonfuls on well buttered baking sheet and bake in a very slow oven (250°) for 30 minutes. If a drier center is desired, they may be baked longer. To make nest shaped meringues to be filled with ice cream, pass the mixture through a star shaped pastry tube onto the buttered baking sheet. Makes 2 dozen large meringues.

BESOS
Mexican Kisses

1 cup shortening   2 cups sifted flour
2 cups sugar   1 teaspoon cinnamon
¼ teaspoon soda

Cream shortening with sugar and work in dry ingredients sifted together. Roll out on slightly floured board about ¼ inch thick and cut into small rounds. Bake in a hot oven (400°) for 10 to 12 minutes. Serve plain or, while kisses are still hot, roll in a mixture of ½ cup sugar and 1 teaspoon powdered cinnamon. About 3 dozen kisses.

TORTA DE GARBANZO
Chick Pea Cake

3 cups cooked garbanzos   1 cup sugar
½ cup milk   ½ teaspoon powdered cinnamon
4 eggs, separated   2 tablespoons whiskey or brandy

Grind or puree the cooked garbanzos and blend with milk. Beat egg yolks well, add sugar, cinnamon and whiskey, and combine with garbanzos. Then fold in stiffly beaten egg whites. Pour into a buttered casserole and bake in a moderate oven (350°) for 1 hour or until center is firm. This recipe may be varied by alternating layers of the garbanzo mixture with layers of thinly sliced pound cake which has been sprinkled with whiskey, and baking, as described above. Serve cold. Torta de Garbanzo resembles a cheese cake.

CHURROS
Mexican Crullers

1 cup sifted flour   1 slice bread
1 teaspoon salt   ½ lemon
1 cup water   Powdered sugar

Sift measured flour 3 times. Add salt to water, heat to the boiling point and immediately pour it into flour all at once, beating mixture until it is fluffy. Pour batter into a pastry tube before it gets cold and drop small amounts about 2 inches long into very hot deep oil in which you have heated the slice of bread and the half lemon until the bread is very dark brown—almost burned—and removed them. When crullers are golden brown remove them to absorbent paper and before they are cold roll in powdered sugar. The burned bread and lemon add a distinctive flavor. Makes 1 dozen crullers.

BORRACHITOS
Little Drunkards (Cookies)

1 cup shortening	½ teaspoon salt
⅔ cup sugar	3 cups sifted flour
2 egg yolks	Claret wine, enough to make
	a soft cookie dough

Cream shortening, add sugar, egg yolks and salt, mixing well. Add flour alternately with wine until all of the flour is used and a soft cookie dough is obtained. Run through a pastry tube in small amounts (or drop from a teaspoon) and bake in a moderately hot oven (375°) from 8 to 10 minutes. Sprinkle cookies with a little sugar and powdered cinnamon as soon as they are removed from the oven. Makes about 6 dozen cookies.

BUNUELOS EN FORMA DE FLOR
Flower Shaped Pastry

4 cups sifted flour	8 eggs
4 teaspoons sugar	¼ cup water
1 teaspoon salt	

Sift all dry ingredients together, then add eggs and water, mixing well and kneading until smooth. Roll out thin on floured board and cut into strips 7 inches long and 2 inches wide. Roll each strip into a cone, pressing the edges together with the fingers so that the dough will hold. Fry in deep hot oil until golden colored and then remove to absorbent paper. These may be rolled in sugar and cinnamon, or honey mixed with a little melted butter may be poured over them as you would syrup. To make extra fancy, sprinkle with pinenuts. Makes 3 dozen bunuelos.

EMPANADAS DE DULCE
Turnovers with Sweet Fillings

Make Empanadas according to either of the basic recipes on page 119, using any of the following fillings: Thick applesauce flavored with cinnamon; jelly; French custard cream; or Cajeta de Camote con Pina on page 107. After Empanadas are baked or fried, and while they are still hot, dip them in a mixture of 1 cup sugar and 1 tablespoon powdered cinnamon.

BUNUELOS
Light-as-a-Feather Mexican Pancakes

3 cups sifted flour	4 eggs
1 tablespoon sugar	1 cup milk
1 teaspoon baking powder	¼ cup butter, melted
1 teaspoon salt	½ cup water, approximately

Sift all dry ingredients together and break eggs into them. Then add milk and butter, and beat mixture well, adding as much water as needed to make a dough that can be easily handled without being sticky. Knead very well and make into balls the size of walnuts, rubbing each ball with shortening to prevent them from sticking. Cover balls with a cloth and let stand 20 minutes. Flour board lightly and roll each ball into a large round, spreading with the hand to make them very thin. Let them stand about 5 minutes, then fry in deep hot oil until golden in color, and remove to absorbent paper to drain. These may be served whole, sprinkled with sugar and cinnamon or with thin honey. The typical Mexican way is to break them into a soup bowl and add a thin syrup made with brown sugar and flavored with stick cinnamon. Makes 2 to 3 dozen bunuelos.

POLVORONES
Mexican Tea Cakes

1 cup butter	¼ teaspoon salt
½ cup confectioners sugar	1 teaspoon vanilla
2¼ cups sifted flour	Confectioners sugar for rolling

Cream butter and add sugar, flour, salt and vanilla, making a moderately stiff dough. Chill in refrigerator for a few hours and then roll into small balls about an inch in diameter. Bake on a buttered cookie sheet in a moderately hot oven (400°) from 14 to 17 minutes. As soon as tea cakes are removed from oven roll them in confectioners sugar. Cool on a wire rack and then roll in sugar again. About 5 dozen

HUEVOS REALES
Royal Eggs

6 egg yolks	1 stick cinnamon
2 cups sugar	Brandy
1 cup water	

Beat egg yolks with a rotary beater for one-half hour. (If you have an electric mixer, use it, of course.) Put into a small, deep baking dish and bake for 45 minutes in a slow oven (300°). Make a moderately thick syrup of the sugar, water and stick cinnamon. Drop the egg by spoonfuls into the hot syrup. When cold, add brandy to taste. Allow to stand about 2 hours until eggs are well soaked with syrup.

116

Chapter Twelve

VARIEDADES -
Miscellaneous

LAS PENAS CON PAN SON MENOS. (You worry less if you eat more.)

VARIEDADES—Miscellaneous

EMPANADAS
Mexican Turnovers

2 cups flour	½ teaspoon salt
2 tablespoons sugar	⅓ cup shortening
2 teaspoons baking powder	⅓ cup ice water (about)

Sift flour, sugar, baking powder and salt into a bowl. Work in the shortening as you would for pastry. Add just enough ice water to hold dough together. Roll out dough on slightly floured board and cut into rounds 3 or 4 inches in diameter. Place a spoonful of filling on one half of the pastry, wet the edge with water, fold the other half of the pastry round over filling and press edges together to seal. Bake* in a moderately hot oven (375°) for 15 to 20 minutes, according to size. Makes about 12 empanadas.

Note: Empanadas may be fried to a golden brown in hot deep fat. Sugar may be omitted from recipe if desired.

Empanada Fillings

Picadillo. See recipe on page 55. Creamed Chicken

Refried beans sprinkled with grated cheese. See recipe on page 100

EMPANADAS
Another recipe

1 package Philadelphia cream cheese, 3 ounces	½ cup butter
	1 cup flour

Cream the butter and cheese together until blended. Add flour and work into a ball. Refrigerate dough over night and remove from refrigerator ½ hour before using. Roll out dough, cut, fill and bake according to directions given in recipe above. These empanadas are nice served with salads. Anchovy paste, deviled ham or a mixture of butter and grated cheese make good fillings.

MEXICAN CHOCOLATE

Mexican chocolate may be bought at any Mexican store. It comes in rounds, each round being marked off into four quarters. Heat the milk then drop in one of these quarters of chocolate for each cup of milk When dissolved, pour the chocolate into a hot pitcher which is to be sent to the table. Then with a *molinillo* (or egg beater), beat vigorously until the chocolate foams. The outstanding flavor of Mexican chocolate is cinnamon. When you are not able to procure the real Mexican chocolate, I would suggest using the American chocolate sparingly and adding a little powdered cinnamon.

COFFEE

Coffee in Mexico is made into a strong extract by the drip method In serving coffee, milk is heated, placed in the cup, and then the coffee extract is added to suit the individual taste. Many persons visiting Mexico from other countries do not like the coffee, because in restaurants it is served full strength, whereas in the homes it is served in the above manner.

TEA

In Mexico tea is made as follows: To the water which you are to use for tea, add stick cinnamon and allow to boil several minutes; then add tea and steep as usual. Do try this; you will find it truly delicious!

CHAMPURRADO

This typical Mexican drink which is commonly served with tamales contains:

Water or milk	Cloves
Brown sugar to taste	Chocolate
Cinnamon	Sufficient masa to thicken

I am not giving proportions because the drink is not likely to have wide appeal.

ATOLE DE CIRUELA

This drink is very commonly used in Sinaloa. It contains the following ingredients:

Water or milk	Cloves
Brown sugar to taste	Soaked dry prunes, which are
Cinnamon	mashed very fine
	Sufficient masa to thicken

This may be varied by adding pineapple juice and omitting the prunes. In this case it is called Atole de Pina.

ATOLE DE MAIZENA

This drink is used for breakfast. To make it, heat milk with a stick of cinnamon for flavor; mix sugar and a little cornstarch with a small amount of cold milk, add to the hot milk and cook until smooth and well blended. Remove cinnamon before serving.

MACARRONES CON JOCOQUI
Macaroni with Sour Cream

1 pound paste (neckties, cut macaroni or other shapes may be used)	1 pound Monterey cream cheese
½ cup butter	1 pint sour cream (2 cups)
	Salt and pepper to taste

Boil macaroni in salted water, drain and run hot water through it. Butter a large casserole. Place a layer of macaroni, dots of butter, cubes of cheese, sprinkle with salt and pepper, and add a layer of sour cream. Repeat this procedure until all ingredients are used, ending with sour cream. Bake, covered, for 30 minutes in a moderately hot oven (350°). Serves 8 to 10. This is a good dish for a large party.

ONE OF MY RECIPES FOR CHILE SAUCE

3 tablespoons butter	1 cup canned tomatoes, passed through sieve
1 onion, minced	
1 green pepper, chopped	1 tablespoon chile powder
1 clove garlic, minced	1 cup beef stock
2 tablespoons flour	Salt and pepper

Fry onion, green pepper and garlic in butter until tender. Then add flour, tomatoes, chile powder dissolved in hot beef stock, and season with salt and pepper. Cook covered for about 15 minutes. This sauce will keep in the refrigerator for approximately one week.

MORE ABOUT ENCHILADAS

Realizing the popularity of this dish among Americans, I am offering a few suggestions which may help the average family to enjoy them in their homes. Flour tortillas may be made by following the recipe given on page 38, and if you do not desire to make chorizo (see page 64) you may use ground beef, seasoned with onion, garlic, salt and pepper and fried before stuffing the enchiladas. The sauce may be simplified by using, instead of the red Mexican chile, a chile sauce which may be bought at any store, diluting it to your individual taste and thickening it with flour. A very tasty sauce may be made in this manner. If you do not desire to have your sauce very hot, tomato sauce may be used to dilute the chile sauce. Then follow the same procedure as given in the enchilada recipe in the book.

PIPIAN
Pumpkin Seed Sauce for Chicken

2 chiles pasilla, from Mexican store
2 chiles anchos, from Mexican store
¾ cup dry pumpkin seeds
½ cup blanched almonds
1 cup popped corn
1 clove garlic
Chicken broth (about 3 cups)
½ cup lard
Salt and pepper

Wash both kinds of chiles and remove seeds; soak pods in warm water to cover for about 20 minutes. Toast pumpkin seeds, almonds, and chile seeds in a dry skillet. Grind all these and the popped corn and garlic to a very fine paste. Mix paste with hot chicken broth, using as much as you desire. Strain and cook the sauce until it thickens like gravy. Remove from heat. Heat lard very hot and add to the above gravy. Return to fire and cook, stirring occasionally, until lard comes to the top. Salt should not be added until the last as the sauce will curdle if it is added earlier. Add fricasseed chicken or turkey to the sauce and heat about 15 minutes before serving. Serves 6.

TWO DELICIOUS DINNERS

●

SOPA DE GARBANZO (Chick Pea Soup)
ENSALADA DE PIMIENTO Y QUESO (Pimiento and Cheese Salad)
ARRECHERA ADOBADA (Barbecued Skirt Steak)
COLECITAS DE BRUSELAS A LA MEXICANA (Brussels Sprouts, Mexican Style)
BORRACHITOS ("Little Drunkards," wine cookies)
Sherbet   Coffee

●

SOPA DE ALBONDIGAS DE PESCADO (Fish Ball Soup)
ENSALADA DE BERENJENAS (Eggplant Salad)
TORTAS DE CAMARON CON NOPALES (Shrimp Fritters with Cactus)
DULCE DE LECHE CON PINA (Mexican Pineapple Milk Pudding)
or
Pressed Quince with Cheese and Crackers   **Coffee**

122

Life at Home
In MEXICO

TENGO UNA HAMBRE QUE PARECE DOS (I'm so hungry, I feel like I'm twins.)

LIFE AT HOME IN MEXICO

*T*o say that the average Mexican family lives in any specified manner, and that its average meals conform to any one pattern would be a gross mis-statement and entirely misleading.

It must be borne in mind that there are different classes or groups of people in Mexico, anyone visiting the country will notice at first glance the striking differentiation as regards personal attire, mode of living, culture, and the like, of various individuals. The mixture of cuisine in Mexico can be explained as follows:

Prior to the conquest of Mexico by Spain which started in 1524 certain traditional foods and methods of preparing them already existed among the Indian tribes; this is corroborated by several historical reports, particularly a chronicle in the form of a diary written by one of the soldiers of Cortez, one Bernal Diaz del Castillo. As an illustration, the present-day tortilla, the pinole, and chocolate, both in the beverage and the candy forms were used by the Mexican Indians long before the Spaniards came.

The Spaniards brought with them their own typical cooking and to this day many of the popular Spanish dishes constitute almost an everyday diet with some Mexican families.

At the time when Mexico attained its independence (1821), foreign investors established themselves in various parts of the country, and thus many of the Mexican people became familiar with American and European dishes.

In the year 1862 Mexico repelled an armed effort on the part of Napoleon III to dominate the country and establish Maximilian of Hapsburg and his wife Charlotte as rulers. During their attempted reign, many French dishes were introduced and accepted.

It is true that the greater portion of the twenty million inhabitants of Mexico are farmers, miners, laborers, and the like who remain in their native towns all their lives, with little opportunity to travel. But it is also true that moneyed and white-collar classes of Mexicans have traveled, acquired culture and therefore learned over a period of many years (generations in some cases) the customs and food habits of other nations. Meanwhile education through schools, movies and radio is rapidly reaching the masses, with the result that everyday home life everywhere is changing.

Then, too, Mexicans in the past two decades have become enthusiastic sportsmen; baseball, football, basketball, polo, tennis, "fronton," swimming, track meets and the like are now popular among young and old throughout the Republic. This is another factor which is affecting Mexican appetites and diets.

It can be seen from the preceding paragraphs that one could not expect to find many families still clinging to old-fashioned routines. In the smaller towns, however, family life even today follows a pattern something like this:

'*A*t daybreak the servants start by sweeping the sidewalk and street in front of the house, following up with the patios, surrounding colonnaded corridors, and the like. Next the kindling wood is lighted on the cooking braziers, charcoal added and coffee started in a clay bowl, while eggs are fetched directly from chicken coops in the yard and held in readiness. The master and lady of the house may then be served a cup or two of coffee with sweetened buns.

"The master of the house then goes to supervise his farm hands in the field; in the meantime the process of rousing the children, bathing and dressing them is being supervised by the wife.

"About 7 a. m. the family sits at table for breakfast which may consist of fruit in season; steak, either fried or broiled, accompanied by fried red beans; followed or preceded by fried eggs, perhaps garnished with a hot chile sauce, all of which is eaten alike by adults and children. Fresh milk may be drunk by the children, while the elders drink hot milk to which has been added a strong, liquid coffee extract.

"The children are then sent to school in care of the nursemaid, and the master sets about his business in town before going back to the fields; in the meantime the beds are being made, the bedrooms tidied, and the general daily house-cleaning gets under way, to end around noon.

"Immediately after breakfast the lady of the house gives the servants instructions as to what must be prepared for the heavy meal of the day, which may be eaten any time between 2 and 4 p. m. Also, while sitting at the table after breakfast, she inspects the accounts given by the servants who did the marketing that morning in the market place.

"While in the fields the master and his men may stop at 11 a. m. for a snack and perhaps a drink of spirits; from the time chosen, this collation derives its name, *las once!*

"ON HIS way home, the master may stop in town and have a drink of tequila; this opportunity is used to discuss with his friends national and international affairs as well as other matters of mutual interest. Meanwhile the children are brought back from school. When the master of the house arrives the heavy meal of the day is served. This meal might well be something like this: broth with cooked vegetables; rice; fish; pork; fried beans; and dessert—perhaps home-made preserves. The children again have fresh milk, while the adults drink beer, wine or *pulque* with the meal; also a small cup of black coffee.

"The whole household sleeps a siesta and around 5 o'clock in the afternoon, hot chocolate and sweetened buns may be partaken by all. This repast is called a *merienda*, a term that has now been adopted to designate a light meal in the early evening, especially in Mexico City.

"After *siesta* and *merienda* the master goes to his business office, the children go with a servant to the movies or indulge in other recreation, and the lady of the house pays social calls.

"The family again sits at the table for supper around 8 p. m. This meal may be a frugal one, but generally the custom is to follow a menu similar to the one used for the heavy meal of the day, though in smaller quantities.

"After the children have had a chance to play in the patio for a while, they are put to bed while the elders listen to the radio or entertain visitors. Around 11 p. m. everybody is in bed.

"Usually there is a big pot of boiled beans in the kitchen from which quantities are taken for frying in order to serve beans at each meal. But aside from beans, no leftovers from a previous meal are served in a subsequent one. Meat prevails in all meals, pork being eaten more frequently than beef. Work goes on constantly in the kitchen from daybreak until far into the night; the washing of dishes is especially hard because, as a general rule, hot water is never used for that purpose.

"Every available opportunity is used by the lady of the house to do sewing, embroidering, knitting, and the like; laundering and ironing go on every day as part of the servants' chores."

In the larger cities, the everyday activities in the average home of the white-collar worker are very similar to those of the average family in the United States. Menus at home differ widely according to the peculiarities developed in each household throughout the preceding generations. In Mexico City, sometimes called the "City of Contrasts," one can find today almost any type of household such as is found in the United States, from the very rich to the very poor, with similar corresponding variations in diets.—

ADIOS, AMIGOS

May your tables be filled with bounty, your days with sunshine, your hearts with joy.

Elena